Death on the Beach

"Deeply compassionate, provokes novel thoughts and fuels introspection." (*Lundagård*)

"That beaches are, on the whole, very bleak places, is convincingly demonstrated in Per Högselius' Death on the Beach, a lovely, compact little collection of essays which gives these playgrounds of horror and sorrow a thorough onceover, through the twin lenses of art and literature." (PETTER LINDGREN IN *Aftonbladet*)

"As an essayist, Högselius is catlike, he moves nimbly and with admirable agility between historical periods and specific examples. Under his treatment, the vastest distances between subjects and genres, times and places shrink. Before you know it, you have travelled very far, very fast without ever noticing… Death on the Beach isn't just an investigative, analytical text. It is also, like all good essays, the product of a distinctive gaze and character: a piece of reality filtered through a temperament." (GUSTAF JOHANSSON IN *TIDSKRIFTEN RESPONS*)

"Högselius' charming musings is one of this captivating book's most outstanding qualities. And as a good essayist, he knows how to balance the universal and the particular, collective culture and private experience, and to add colour to the contours of historical examples with the help of his own personal experiences and unique memories." (MARTIN LAGERHOLM IN *SVENSKA DAGBLADET*)

The clichéd images of beach sunsets and seaside summer homes fade like sun-bleached wallpaper against the dark coastal horrors Högselius presents in his collection of beach finds from our cultural history. The strength of this book: even though it ranges through the geography of our planet, it doesn't primarily arouse a yen to travel, but to read." (ANNA BLENNOW IN *SYDSVENSKAN*)

ABOUT THE AUTHOR

PER HÖGSELIUS grew up in Stockholm, Sweden. As a child he dreamed about becoming an astronomer, which led him to study physics at university. In his teens he discovered palaeontology, history and literature. A hopeless romantic, he wished he had lived in the nineteenth century. He became a passionate traveller, targeting not so much the distant corners of the world but the nearby post-Cold War lands of the Baltic Sea region. His journeys there became the basis for his first non-academic book in Swedish, the historical travelogue *Östersjövägar* (Baltic Sea Paths, 2007). Later on, he fell in love with the North Sea and subsequently with China. Meanwhile Per has pursued an academic career in the history of science, technology and environment. A professor at KTH Royal Institute of Technology in Stockholm, he enjoys juxtaposing different genres and styles of writing in exploring human experiences with technology and nature. He writes regularly for the leading Swedish daily *Svenska Dagbladet*.

ABOUT THE TRANSLATOR

AGNES BROOMÉ has a PhD in Translation Studies from University College London. Her translations include August Prize winners *The Expedition* by Bea Uusma, *The Gospel of the Eels* by Patrik Svensson, and *Collected Works* by Lydia Sandgren, and the 2022 Petrona Award winner Maria Adolfsson's *Fatal Isles*. She is director of the Scandinavian Studies program at Harvard.

Death on the Beach

Essays from a Marginal World

PER HÖGSELIUS

Translated by AGNES BROOMÉ

BARB
ICAN
PRESS

Published by Barbican Press, Los Angeles and London
© Per Högselius, 2024
English Translation © Agnes Broomé, 2024

First published in Swedish as *Döden på stranden*, Ellerströms
förlag, 2020. This first English edition has been revised from
the Swedish original, and includes additional chapters.

US office: 1032 19th Street, Unit 2, Santa Monica CA90403
Registered UK office: 1 Ashenden Road, London E5 0DP

www.barbicanpress.com
@barbicanpress1

Cover photo by Zane Lee: Unsplash

Cover design by Jason Anscomb

Library of Congress Control Number: 2023945349

A CIP catalogue for this book is available from the British Library

Typeset by Tetragon, London
Distributed in North America by Publishers Group West

ISBN: 978-1-909954-95-3

Contents

Preface

As far back as I can remember, I've been drawn to beaches. The beaches of my childhood belonged to Lake Mälaren, their sand dark and coarse. My mother anxiously watched over me as I played at the water's edge. Further out, there was a shipping lane where large boats passed by. I wasn't allowed to swim out that far.

When I was eleven, we took a family holiday on Gotland, the large island in the middle of the Baltic Sea. There, we stumbled across Kvarnåkershamn, a small village where several plots of land were for sale in the coastal pine forest. The cottage my parents quickly had built became my fixed point during the summers that followed. It's where I met my first love and lost myself in longing. But when I was alone, I roved the shingle beaches in search of fossils. The rocks were full of long-since extinct plants and animals: crinoids, corals, trilobites. I dreamed of becoming a palaeontologist, dedicating my days to these creatures that once were.

As it happened, however, my scientific career never really took off. Instead, I increasingly turned my gaze to the sea, towards the foreign beaches hidden somewhere beyond the horizon. After the fall of the Soviet Union, I went to see them. I took to writing about the Baltic Sea region and its eventful past. I was struck by how our new, optimistic era – in which we were said to have reached the end of history – contrasted with the physical state of the Baltic's eastern shores: they were desolately dirty, littered with debris from the Cold War Era. Rumour had it mines were still buried in the sand.

Many years later, I settled in the Netherlands for a while. I wandered the beaches of the North Sea, my daily routine governed by the rhythm of the tide. I still remember the silhouettes of the freight ships out at sea, lying at anchor as they waited to dock in Rotterdam. At the beach cafés, I listened to stories of capsized ships and beached whales. I thought about Doggerland, once a favourite grazing ground for woolly mammoths between the Netherlands and the UK, now swallowed by the sea.

Beaches are places of mystery and contradiction. And over time, I've come to see more of their dark side, not only in my own explorations, but also through my encounters with the seashore in literature, film, art, and music – as well as in the daily reports from every corner of the world relayed to me by the newspapers.

Where does it come from, this dark side? Is there a way to find out? I remember a faded old photograph my mother once showed me. She's standing on a Black Sea beach, a smiling young woman, with her arms around a tall, lanky man who is about to become my father. She doesn't know it yet: that she's pregnant. That a child is growing inside her. The sea glitters behind them, the sea that was named for blackness, even though it's so blindingly bright in the summer sun.

I

Caravaggio

The idea of the beach as a zone of death, fear and sorrow first took root in me many years ago during a visit to Whitby, one of my favourite destinations on the east coast of England. One evening, while strolling through the picturesque town, I happened to pass by a flea market. Having bought three beautiful seashells, I made a more unexpected find. It was a DVD, a film, succinctly entitled *Caravaggio*. The director, an Italian I had never heard of by the name of Angelo Longoni, had, as far as I could make out, made the film for Italian television. How a copy of his biopic had made its way to that flea market, I have no idea, but there it was in front of me, in a damp cardboard banana box from the Caribbean. The off-putting cover – featuring Caravaggio's severed head, as depicted by the artist himself in a famous painting – did not deter me from purchasing the disc. That evening, I fed it into the DVD player in my hotel room. While one of the winter's first storms swept in from the North Sea, blasting Whitby with freezing brine, I watched Caravaggio's journey through life.

I particularly recall the ending. The artist, portrayed by the imposing Alessio Boni, is at the peak of his creative life.

He is only thirty-eight years old but can already look back at an exceptional career. He has single-handedly revolutionised Italian painting with his idiosyncratic lighting and dramatic style. His art already graces countless new churches and private villas – in Rome and Naples, on Sicily and Malta. The elite covet his works. But he is also infamous for his wild ways and temperament. In several parts of the country, he is wanted for various violent deeds. Now he lives an itinerant life, on the run from his enemies.

Then, in July of 1610, he is reached by the news that Pope Paul V has decided to pardon him. He is beside himself with joy. Finally, he will be able to return to his beloved Rome! In Chiaia outside Naples, he boards a felucca that will take him to Palo, a border post near the mouth of the Tiber. Some of his most recent works – gifts for the pope – are in his luggage. The first leg of the journey goes according to plan. But when Caravaggio arrives in Palo and shows his identity documents, he is denied entry to the papal state. The master

is stunned. "But I have been pardoned!" he protests. He is apprehended and taken to a jail cell. At the same time, the ship that brought him casts off – and disappears out to sea. With his paintings still on board.

That night, Caravaggio is plagued by terrible nightmares portending a fever. The next morning, he's not himself, raving and staring around in confusion. A papal representative arrives and explains that the detention was an unfortunate mistake, that the commanding officer in Palo simply hadn't heard about the pardoning. Now, the paintings have to be recovered before they fall into the wrong hands. "The ship you arrived on is on its way to Porto Ercole," the papal representative tells Caravaggio, leading him to a small fishing vessel headed for the same destination. "Don't worry, you'll catch up with them."

But in the leaden heat out at sea, Caravaggio's illness becomes more pronounced. The fishermen soon realise he's in a bad way. They exchange worried looks. "He's going to die!" they exclaim to each other. One thought quickly leads to another. "We have to get rid of him before he dies on board!" Having thus decided, they turn into a sandy bay – and heave the sick man over the railing. There's a splash as the body lands in the surf. Sick as he is, Caravaggio is only vaguely aware of what's happening. He slowly crawls through rotting seaweed, apparently unaware of his surroundings. While the fishing boat sets sail again and disappears out to sea, he staggers up onto the beach – but he is too weak and collapses. The beach is deserted. The July sun is searing. Caravaggio's own paintings flash before his eyes: Goliath's severed but still living head, which is really a self-portrait, and the large altarpiece in the Knights of Malta's chapel in Valletta, depicting John the Baptist, who has also been beheaded and from whose neck blood is gushing.

Slowly, he struggles onto his feet. As he straightens up, he sees a black stallion, carrying a rider dressed all in black. The rider has no face. The animal rears up and flails its hooves wildly in the scorching sand. It whinnies furiously and starts galloping toward Caravaggio. He tries to shake off the hallucination. But the rider closes in on him. Caravaggio desperately leaps aside, slips in the seaweed, loses his balance, and falls to ground. Where he remains. The stallion reaches the lifeless body, studies it, whinnies one final time – and walks away.

Back in Whitby, it was late by the time the film ended. I turned off the DVD player and returned to my own reality. The Mediterranean sun faded and instead the North Sea storm demanded my attention as it redoubled its efforts. It ripped and tore at the small town, as though it wanted to pull it down into the briny ocean depths. The hotel windows rattled ominously and when I looked out I saw giant waves flash in the light from the harbour floodlights. I felt ill at ease. I lay down on the bed, but sleep would not come. Lying awake for hours, I listened to the gale, thought about life and pondered Caravaggio's cruel fate.

I recalled that Caravaggio's death was a contentious subject among art historians, that in fact very little was known about his last few days – and about how his life ended. Some felt certain he was not only deceived, as the film would have it, but murdered, possibly poisoned. Others were convinced he was killed in Naples, possibly in a knife fight, or after contracting malaria. The latest contribution to this debate had been a DNA analysis that purported to prove that certain bodily remains discovered in a church in Porto Ercole were in fact Caravaggio's. But how and when they were interred there remained a mystery.

At the same time, I couldn't help but think the filmmakers had hit the nail on the head when they had Caravaggio meet his doom on a sun-scorched Mediterranean beach. Longoni's interpretation seemed anything but far-fetched, particularly in light of humankind's historical relationship with the sea. Because there was no doubt Caravaggio had lived in a time when the seashore was generally perceived as exactly that: a territory of death. It had been a landscape that evoked fear and repulsion, an eerie and ominous zone that signalled danger – and which was therefore avoided whenever possible.

In Alain Corbin's book *The Lure of the Sea*, which in bookshops was shelved under non-fiction, but which could just as easily have been placed in the horror section, I had read about how a "veil of repulsive images" – drawn from the Bible in particular – had made it virtually impossible for sixteenth and seventeenth century Europeans to approach the seashore with any measure of enjoyment. Fear had taken root as early as the Judeo-Christian myth of creation with its vision of a plunging "deep" – a dark, inhospitable water over which the Spirit of God hovered in the beginning. The ocean, contemporary theologians claimed, was what remained of this abyss. Its function was to remind Christians of the world as it had been before Creation – a terrifying place – and of the fact that

Creation itself was incomplete. The Book of Job said that the Lord, like a modern water engineer, "shut up the sea with doors" and gave it "a decreed place". That place was bounded by the shore. "Hitherto shalt thou come, but no further!" he had told the sea. "Here shall thy proud waves be stayed!" The sea had symbolised the endless and unfathomable – to such a degree that it had bordered on blasphemy to even gaze out at the unbroken horizon. Lena Lenček, another shore historian well worth reading, claims the sea was generally viewed as a cursed realm in whose darkness grotesque creatures devoured each other and the forces of Hell reigned unchallenged. Unhappy souls, the kind that found no peace in death, were thought to lurk in the depths. It is no coincidence that the symbolic topography in Dante's *Inferno* bears such close resemblance to a maelstrom. In the Garden of Eden, on the other hand, there existed no ocean and no shoreline.

The most terrifying of all Biblical narratives was the one about the Flood, in which God used the sea to punish humanity and destroy all life on Earth – apart from Noah and the few chosen creatures allowed onto the Ark. Hearing that story would hardly have filled anyone with a longing to head down to the seashore – where utter destruction had once begun. A common view among scientists at the time was that the coastal landscape, with its vast sandy beaches, clattering shingles, strange rock formations and dramatic bluffs could not be explained as anything but a direct consequence of this tragedy. What they felt they saw in the coastal landscape was desolation, bearing undeniable witness to what had once come to pass. The seashore was a realm of catastrophe and chaos – and in the eyes of baroque Europe therefore also an ugly, inaesthetic landscape.

The fierce storms intermittently whipped up by the sea also seemed to portend more floods to come. Some were so

overcome by fear at this idea that the mere sight of the ocean could provoke hysteria about the world's impending doom. True, the Book of Revelation tells us the apocalypse will come through fire rather than water – but a commonly held view was that it would be preceded by the seas running amok: water would inundate the mountains and fish and sea monsters would come to the surface, emitting awful noises as the skies were set aflame.

These Biblical fantasies were amplified and verified by the – highly subjective – European reading of Ancient Greek and Roman texts. The intellectuals of the sixteenth and seventeenth centuries trembled before the sea and its wrath as it was expressed in for example *The Odyssey*, *The Aeneid* and many other works. It was primarily these literatures, rather than their own experiences, that inspired the marine narratives of the new age – such as the description of the storm in Rabelais' *The Life of Gargantua and of Pantagruel*, to name one typical example. At the same time, they dreaded the many dangers that, in the classical texts, lurked on the shore itself. Greek and Roman tradition held that the seashore was teeming with hostile creatures of lore, led by the rock monster Scylla, with her six hideous dog heads, and the crafty Charybdis, a vortex that devoured and disgorged its victims. Venturing onto the shore, one also risked affliction by various strange diseases. Intellectual giants such as Strabo, Seneca and Pliny the Elder all claimed the sea was a continual source of "purification", because it pushed all kinds of impurities up onto its beaches. This was why, they asserted, many beaches, particularly those of the Mediterranean, emitted such a foul stench.

In the seventeenth century, Europeans still believed amber was a form of oceanic excretion and that the foam on the crests of waves was the sweat of brininess. On the whole, beaches were viewed as a place of putrefaction. The theory seemed to chime well with actual experiences of waterborne plagues which – with the Bubonic Plague of the fourteenth century as the most terrifying example – had periodically made it literally impossible to inhabit the coast from the Middle Ages onward. Sixteenth and seventeenth century doctors firmly discouraged their patients from visiting beaches. Rumour had it Death himself walked abroad there. For some, he came in the shape of a black rider. For others, he sat among the rocks, waiting to play chess, as in Ingmar Bergman's *The Seventh Seal*.

And so, Europeans avoided spending time in the immediate vicinity of the ocean. Those who, for one reason or another,

had no choice but to live on its shores built their houses so they wouldn't have to look at it; with their windows facing land rather than the blue waves. The seashore was primarily the domain of the poorest: fishermen and salt workers, beach riders and lighthouse keepers, witches and whores. The only people who willingly sought it out were religious seekers, who had made meditating on life, the world and God their life's mission. Holy women and men settled down at the edge of the ocean, preferably on lonely, brutally inaccessible coasts such as Atos in the Aegean Sea and Orkney in the North Atlantic – to seek their Creator in terror. Here, on the outskirts of civilisation, with an unobscured view of the horror of the sea, they could come closer to God than anywhere else, and during their solitary walks along the beaches, they could study the traces left by the Flood. They sought out the shore in the same spirit that other extremists lay down on beds of nails or walked through fire – it was about accepting suffering, about enduring pain, about self-flagellation as a path to cleansing one's soul and achieving clarity. There was nothing joyful about the shore.

All this changed, if historians like Corbin and Lenček are to be believed, in the years between 1750 and 1840. Over the course of these decades, Europeans pushed aside the veil of repulsive images – and learned to long for the sea. People from north-western Europe in particular came to re-evaluate the shoreline. The coastland was fundamentally transformed as strings of seaside resorts blossomed. England – with Scarborough and Brighton as especially desirable destinations – led the way. People travelled there when the cities became too oppressive and older inland spa towns lost their allure. A new generation of physicians began to prescribe seaside stays for the sick, who now, contrary to the medical advice of yore, were encouraged to go sea bathing, take walks along the beach and drink a pint of seawater a day. The healthy soon came flocking, too. They came to enjoy the cool sea air, admire the views, study nature, mingle with fishermen and socialise with their peers. They were soon joined by the Romantics, who rediscovered the depth of the human soul in the water's reflection and used the resorts as their base as they went in search of adventure along the coast in the spirit of Robinson Crusoe. Starting in the middle of the nineteenth century, when the first railway lines were built from the cities down to the coast, the masses became able to visit the sea resorts, too. At that point, there was no way back: modern beach life had become part of Western society for good.

I am, however, personally not entirely convinced the Europeans' relationship with the seashore has changed quite as radically as Corbin and Lenček claim. I find it difficult to put my finger on it, but something about this narrative doesn't fit. At least that was what I thought to myself when a few days later, back in Stockholm, I unpacked the seashells I had bought at Whitby's flea market. Unwrapping the old newspaper that the stallholder had provided to protect the shells, I stared in disbelief at one of the headlines:

ARTIST STARVES TO DEATH ON SCOTTISH BEACH

The artist in question was a woman, Margaret Davies, who had been thirty-nine years old – the same age as Caravaggio.

She had met her fate in Kearvaig, a sandy bay near the isolated Cape Wrath on Scotland's west coast. Two months earlier, in September 2002, she had left her home in Danbury in Essex, travelling to Inverness by coach and continuing from there on foot – even though she'd walked with a severe limp since childhood – through the wild Highlands. On the way, she had found the time to paint and write. She had crossed Scotland from east to west. In Kearvaig, she had found shelter in a small beach cottage. And there she had remained.

Her body had been discovered a few days later by a shepherd come to round up his sheep. From the heathland on the cape, he had driven the animals down toward Kearvaig. There, he had noticed the door to the white cottage standing wide open. Inside, he had discovered the artist, curled up in her sleeping bag in one of the rough-hewn beds. Her body had been so emaciated and withered it had brought to mind victims of famine in the world's poorest countries. The fireplace held the charred remains of burnt driftwood. Outside the cabin, the Atlantic roared in its full majesty.

Why had Margaret Davies met her fate on the beach? Why hadn't she left that desolate place to look for help? There were, once again, no shortage of theories. Some speculated that she had belonged to an Australian cult whose members believed they could live off air alone. Another hypothesis posited that she had staged her own death – that it was in fact a performance piece, a work of art. Neither explanation seemed to account for the desperation she expressed in her travel journal – unless she was deliberately searching for that desperation? "She liked to experience hardships", her mother commented. "She did actually like the cold. I think she was camping on the beach. She had left a note at the bothy saying she was on the beach, running out of food."

2

The Beach Killer

Countless are they, the people who for one reason or another –
or for no reason at all – have met their fate on the beach.
Some have perished in mass tragedies, like when a tsunami
hits, destroying everything in its path, or when a foreign fleet
arrives and massacres the population of a coastal city. Others
have faced their shore doom – as conjured by the forces of
darkness or light – alone: sometimes accidentally, sometimes
intentionally, sometimes along the harsh path of violence.

Thinking about the beach as a zone of violence, I remember
a visit to the Stockholm City Library a year or so ago. I was
putting the finishing touches to a scholarly article, intended
for publication, on the theme of eutrophication as a historic
phenomenon. The last part of my paper, or so I had planned,
would be about how this very serious environmental threat
has been expressed in fiction. One of my search terms was
"släke", a regional Swedish word for rotting sea wrack. To my
surprise, I found in the library's database a book of fiction
that not only related to this concept, but that had taken the
word as its title. The author was Håkan Östlundh.
Unfortunately, I had difficulty locating the book physically.

It was not to be found on any of the library's shelves. Nor had it been put in stores. After asking a librarian, I was finally directed to a strange little room I had never noticed before, even though I've been a regular at the library for many years. It was discreetly located between the main hall and one of the non-fiction rooms. The space was windowless, aside from a tiny aperture in the far corner, and the lighting rather dim. At the entrance, someone had placed a bronze statue depicting a rough-hewn, seated man who seemed to keep watch over the room; it was Swedish poet Gunnar Ekelöf. After a moment's hesitation, I entered.

This was where I found the book. To my disappointment, however, it turned out to be a mere crime novel – a genre I loathe. Nor did it contain any references to eutrophication as an environmental problem. Instead, the book was about gruesome murders and grotesque human remains discovered on the beaches of Gotland. The first body, a man, was found as early as page seven: it was hidden in a roof box on a Volvo parked by a public beach. The police opened the box and found that the body was "cut open from the throat to the groin". The stench was unbelievable; it mingled with the putrid reek of the rotting seaweed on the beach.

I closed Östlundh's book, determined not to borrow it under any circumstances. It wasn't just uninteresting, it was repugnant. I couldn't for the life of me understand how anyone would willingly read such nonsense. That being said, I lingered for a while in the dimly lit, windowless room, which was dedicated exclusively to crime novels and thrillers. I looked around, curious in spite of myself. I hadn't borrowed or bought a crime novel since I was a schoolboy. What is it that draws so many readers to this bizarre genre of literature? I asked myself while I flipped through some of the volumes. And why were so many of them set in coastal regions, in the immediate vicinity of the sea? I picked up a book by Viveca Sten, *Still Waters*, which someone had carelessly tossed on a book cart. It takes place in Stockholm's archipelago. In the introduction, a man is walking his dog on a beach. It's early morning: "Those living in the few houses along the shoreline had hardly woken up. The only sound came from the screaming gulls. The air was fresh and clear, the overnight rain had given everything a newly washed feel". But then the dog is suddenly nowhere to be found. Where has it got to? The man can hear it barking in the distance. At length, he finds it standing over by a big rock, sniffing something.

He went over to have a look, noticing an unpleasant smell.
As he got closer, it turned into a sour, suffocating miasma.

On the ground lay something that looked like a bundle of old rags.

He bent down to shoo the dog away and realized it was an old fishing net full of seaweed. Suddenly, he understood what he was seeing.

The fishing net ended in two bare feet, both of which were missing several toes. Only bones protruded from what was left of the shriveled, greenish skin.

Before he could stop himself, his stomach turned inside out. A surge of pink vomit poured out and splashed his shoes.

The room also held a full set of Wallander novels. I opened one of them at random; it was called *The Dogs of Riga*. The story opens with an anonymous phone call to the Ystad Police, in southern Sweden, on a cold November night. A man's voice claims a red life raft with two dead men inside is about to drift ashore somewhere along the coast of Skåne. And true enough, the next morning, a woman who has gone out for a walk on the fictional Mossby Beach comes across the raft. The woman calls the police and Detective Kurt Wallander gets in his car. He drives along the sea, shuddering at the sight of the breaking waves. When he reaches his destination, he finds the beach woefully abandoned. The red raft is bobbing at the water's edge, stuck between rocks by a long wooden jetty. The dead men are already decomposing. The winter cold and the strong winds do nothing to keep the unmistakable smell of corpse from reaching Wallander.

The more I looked around that out-of-the-way room at the library, the more astonished I felt at the number of crime novels set by the sea. Beach deaths in this by now very diverse literary genre – as in the closely related horror and fantasy genres – seemed to constitute a virtual epidemic: it ravaged practically every coast on the planet and not one crime writer seemed immune to its dark siren call. Something about the seashore clearly makes it an ideal place, an ideal landscape, for the staging of sudden, violent death.

Why this would be so was not immediately clear to me. The simplest explanation was perhaps that the authors had decided to exploit the inherent tension between paradise and hell, between dream and nightmare, or – since we're talking about water – between the bright, clean surface of this world and its dark, murky depths. The beach is a place where we normally experience happiness and pleasure, where we can, like nowhere else, relax and enjoy life in its purest form – and the discovery of a corpse in this environment therefore effectively creates that sense of shock all crime writers make a living giving their readers.

But this, I surmised, was only half the truth. Looking deeper, far from all crime novels painted the seashore as a fundamentally friendly and happy place. It was just as common for beaches to be depicted as intrinsically ominous landscapes. Many of the bodies found by the sea in the world of crime fiction were not discovered by holidaymakers or sun worshippers, but rather on deserted beaches in remote, desolate locations and preferably during the colder seasons. The wanderer who comes across the body is usually alone. She studies the lifeless bundle, trying to understand what she's looking at. Then she looks up and scans the horizon. The air is filled with the screeching of seabirds.

The waves keep rolling in as though nothing has happened, a low, monotonous rumble. The wanderer wants to scream, and then she does – but who can hear her? She is overcome with horror and vertigo. She feels small, infinitely small under the overcast sky, before the endless, rough sea. Once again, she studies the body on the ground, half covered in seashells, seaweed, briny sand. And she can feel the resonance: between nature, wild and cruel, and the primitive violence we humans have again and again shown ourselves capable of.

In this sense the crime literature echoes an ancient, pre-modern fear.

On the Tyrrhenian coast, not far from Naples, there is a small, unremarkable port city by the name of Salerno. Long ago, it was the capital of a duchy with the same name. In the eleventh century, the duchy was ruled by a prince called Guaimar IV. Born in 1013, he was only fourteen years old when he succeeded his father as the regent of Salerno. He would spend the larger part of the rest of his life waging bloody wars of conquest. He threw his lot in with the fierce Normans, who appeared in Italy from a number of directions around the turn of the millennium. He seized control of Capua, Amalfi and Sorrento in the south and Gaeta and nearby territories in the north. Naples, too, was eventually incorporated into Guaimar's realm. Later, he set his sights on Apulia on the Italian peninsula's opposite coast and Calabria on its "toe". Here, however, he became embroiled in a complicated feudal power struggle that marked the beginning of the end of his triumphs.

The setbacks began in earnest in 1047, when the Holy Roman Emperor Henry III and the armies under his command turned against Guaimar. The Emperor recaptured Capua and several other duchies on behalf of their previous regents. Guaimar lost control of Apulia and Calabria. In addition, at a synod in Benevento in 1051, Pope Leo IX demanded that he put a stop to the Norman attacks against the Holy See's territory, which he had been known to encourage. Guaimar ignored this request. Early the next summer, the bell tolled for his dominion. People had had enough of his warlike reign, even back home in Salerno. Powerful people in his inner circle, eagerly urged on by his enemies in the region, conspired against the prince. The end was nigh. Perhaps he could sense what awaited him. We do not know why he sought refuge on the seashore on that sunny June day in the year of 1052. But on that day, writes a contemporary chronicler, "Prince Guaimar was murdered on the seashore through a conspiracy of the Amalfians, whom he had treated very badly, his brothers-in-law and certain inhabitants of Salerno." It was a horrifying deed. "He was run through with thirty-six wounds, suffered great indignities and was dragged along the seashore for some time in quite a disgraceful way." The city of Salerno and its citadel were then captured by his killers.

Guaimar's fate is known to posterity because he was a powerful person. The brief yet detailed description in the chronicle makes it possible for us to imagine his life and pity him for the gruesome death that awaited him. But Guaimar was far from the only person of his time to meet his maker on a beach. Over the course of those tumultuous centuries,

artists – Christianity as sham. He concerned himself with social injustice, with the poor, the vulnerable and oppressed, with robbers and bandits – people who, in his opinion, were not to blame for the situation they found themselves in. What these people needed wasn't a stronger faith but, rather, fairer treatment in society. This view – a controversial one to say the least in this era of religious strife – is clearly expressed in his art. His self-assumed mission as an artist became to evoke – and reveal – the world as it really was, Italian society the way he experienced and understood it. And it was on the periphery – socially and geographically – that this unvarnished, bleak and dangerous world was best depicted. The result is a unique body of work in which the coastal landscapes of the Mediterranean play a key role. Two of Rosa's most well-known works are *View of the Gulf of Salerno* (1645) – which is to say the onetime domains of Guaimar – and *Bandits on a Rocky Coast* (1656).

In the eighteenth century, long after Rosa's death, his art experienced an unexpected renaissance. His paintings spread through Europe by means of reproduction, not least to England, where Italy had become fashionable. English observers took particular note of the dramatic landscapes in Rosa's paintings; in time, they would prove a pivotal influence on romantic marine and landscape painters like Turner. They also fired the imagination of many authors, among others a young woman by the name of Ann Radcliffe, who was on the cusp of achieving considerable fame herself. Radcliffe never had the chance to visit Italy, nor did she need to since Salvator Rosa's art provided perfect settings for the stories she wanted to tell. And so, she set her fiction in Italy.

Radcliffe's novel *The Italian*, which was published in 1797, is a typical example of what the result could be. It opens with balmy evenings on the safe shores of the Bay of Naples, but soon takes an eerie turn as the scene is moved to much bleaker coasts. At the heart of the plot are the young orphan Ellena di Rosalba and a hot-livered noble by the name of Vincentio di Vivaldi, who are head over heels in love with each other. Vivaldi's mother is firmly opposed to the match, but Radcliffe allows her young lovers to defy her and, even worse, the mighty Catholic Church. Their punishment is swift and severe. Vivaldi's mother is persuaded by her counsellor, the sinister and manipulative monk Schedoni, to have Ellena murdered. But how? And *where* should such a deed be attempted? Schedoni has a concrete suggestion:

> On the shore of the Adriatic, in the province of Apulia, not far
> from Manfredonia, is a house that might suit the purpose. It is

a lone dwelling on the beach, and concealed from travellers,
among the forests, which spread for many miles along the coast.

Schedoni makes sure Ellena is kidnapped and taken to the
cottage on the beach. She's received by the monk's accom-
plice Spalatro, a local fisherman. The terrified young woman
is brought to a bare and stuffy room. The door is locked. She
walks over to the barred window, gazes out at the sea, listening
to its rumbling song. The moon rises, illuminating the crests
of the waves. She thinks about her beloved and ponders her
cruel fate.

The next night, she's allowed to walk on the beach. The
thought of escape occurs to her. But then she spots a figure
in a dark cloak approaching from a rocky outcrop. Schedoni
has arrived. The sea is vast and dark, the air vibrating with
the shrill screeching of gulls. Threatening clouds loom at the
horizon. Schedoni has a dagger concealed under his monk's
robe. It is time for the deed.

Radcliffe was a pioneer in the genre that would eventually
become known as Gothic romance. Over the course of the
nineteenth century, the genre evolved in new, unexpected
directions, but the pull of the sea remained an obligatory
component in almost every work written. It is, for example,
no coincidence that Mary Shelley's *Frankenstein* (1818), like
several of Radcliffe's novels, reaches its narrative climax on the
seashore. In this case, the scene is set in the far north, in the
mist-shrouded lands of Scotland and Ireland. Frankenstein,
the eccentric scientist, has sought refuge on Orkney, where he
has turned a fisherman's cottage into a laboratory. During the

day, he busies himself with hair-raising experiments, at night he walks along the water's edge, pondering human existence and listening to the crashing of the Atlantic. Here, he also comes to his fateful decision: to not make any more creatures of the kind he awoke from lifeless matter in the German town of Ingolstadt. The male monster, the product of those activities, has threatened to kill his maker's loved ones unless he agrees to make it a female partner. But Frankenstein cannot abide the thought of a monster couple that could reproduce and spread its offspring across the Earth. He revolts against himself, in a sense, and in a fit of rage he destroys the female monster body waiting for the spark of life in his seaside laboratory. When night comes, he gathers up the fleshy remains of it, places them in a basket laden with heavy rocks and carries the whole thing down to the shore, where a boat awaits. By the light of the full moon, he steers out to sea, heaves the basket overboard – and then lets the waves rock him to sleep.

Revenge is swift. When Frankenstein arrives in Ireland the next day, having been brought by the ocean currents, he's told the body of a young man has been found on the beach. The man has not drowned; his clothes are dry. "He had apparently been strangled, for there was no sign of any violence except the black mark of fingers on his neck." Seeing the body is a severe shock for Frankenstein: the victim is Percival, his best friend. And there can be no doubt who the killer is.

The seashore is a borderland, a marginal world that resists integration into standard geographies. The moment we leave the seaside resorts behind, we enter a zone in which modern rules have been erased and dark forces given free rein. Anything can happen there. Radcliffe and Shelley sensed that and used it in their tales of horror. Modern crime authors follow in their bloody footsteps.

But their works are not pure imagination; deadly violence does in fact also run rampant along many coasts. The media reports almost daily on the most horrifying acts of violence committed by the sea – acts that in their brutality often surpass what Guaimar IV endured in the eleventh century or what literary characters like Schedoni or Frankenstein's monster proved themselves capable of. Most seem utterly meaningless, like when a girl was recently stabbed to death on a South African beach after refusing to hand over her mobile phone to a group of criminal youths, or when a tractor driver mowed down an old homeless man on a public beach in New Jersey. In some cases, the murders have been political. Socialist leader Jean-Pierre Deteix in New Caledonia and opposition politician Jeremias Pondeca in Mozambique, both shot dead on beaches in their respective home countries, count among the latest victims in this category. Beach murders connected to criminal gangs and organised crime are also common, like in the autumn of 2003 when Joe Urdiales was attacked by four hard-boiled men in a supermarket in Texas. The group was led by a member of the Hitler-inspired Aryan Brotherhood. They forced the Spanish-speaking Urdiales, himself a member of a notorious prison gang, into a car and drove down to the stunningly beautiful Padre Island National Seashore, a national park on the Gulf of Mexico. When they reached the beach, the victim was forced to eat sand. Then he was stabbed. His remains were discovered six days later by park rangers.

The most infamous beach murders in modern times are the ones that for several years shook Long Island, to whose beaches New Yorkers flock to soak up the sun and swim in the sea. The main thoroughfare from New York to the more sparsely populated areas in the north east, the Ocean Parkway, hugs the shoreline. This was where tragedy struck in the spring of 2010. The police received a phone call from a sex worker, a woman by the name of Shannan Gilbert. She had spent the evening with a client in Oak Beach, about an hour and a half from New York. Now, night had fallen. The sound of the Atlantic was deafening. When she called, she believed she was being followed by someone who wanted to kill her. While she waited for the police to come, she desperately banged the doors of several beach houses, but no one opened. In the end, she ran into the night and disappeared.

In the days that followed, the police mounted a frantic search for Gilbert – to no avail. But then, six months later, there was a macabre discovery: by the side of the road near Gilgo Beach, not far from Oak Beach, a plastic bag turned out to contain the skeleton of a young woman. When the police scoured the surrounding area, they found the remains of three more women. All had been dead for some time. In the spring of 2011, four more bodies were found, this time slightly further east along the Ocean Parkway. Two of them were female, the third belonged to a man and the fourth was a toddler. Later on, parts of another body – pieces of a cranium, two hands and a lower arm – were found near Jones Beach State Park, and not far from there another cranium and two teeth.

The first four women to have been found were quickly identified. None of them was Shannan Gilbert. But they were all roughly her age and, like her, sex workers. Their names were Maureen, Melissa, Megan and Amber and they were between twenty-two and twenty-seven years old. They had been reported missing between 2007 and 2010. Some of the other victims, including the man, who had been wearing women's clothing, were also found to have been sex workers. The police were also able to identify the two victims who had not been found intact. One of the two craniums turned out to belong to a murdered woman whose severed legs had washed up on nearby Fire Island as early as 1996, while the other matched a dismembered body discovered forty-five miles from Gilgo Beach in the summer of 2003.

All cases remain unsolved. The police believe there is a single perpetrator. He is called the "Long Island Serial Killer" – or, in the succinct manner of the locals: the "Beach Killer".

3

Medusa

Across the Atlantic from Long Island, where the Beach Killer is still on the loose, lies a shallow African bay. The Bay of Arguin, as it is called, is well-known in ornithological circles, because millions of migratory birds gather there to mate. Seafarers, on the other hand, have never had much good to say about its sandy waters; well aware as they are of the hundreds of ships that have run aground one of its treacherous shoals and sunk over the years.

One of those ships was a French frigate that went by the ominous name of Medusa. In the summer of 1816, she was on her way from France to West Africa. The objective was to re-establish the French colony Senegal, which the English had annexed halfway through the eighteenth century, but the Congress of Vienna had returned to the French that year. Aboard the Medusa were over 400 people, of which 160 formed her crew. The intended Senegalese governor, Colonel Julien-Désirée Schmaltz, wanted to reach the colonial port of Saint Louis in record time. He therefore persuaded the Medusa's captain to cut across the Bay of Arguin. Schmaltz believed the reported dangers of the bay had been exaggerated, and the captain didn't dare to disagree. In the distance, they could just make out Cape Blanc, a familiar sight to sailors in those parts and a supposedly reliable landmark on the border between modern Western Sahara and Mauritania. Unfortunately, it was a mirage: what they saw was in fact nothing more than a cloudbank. When Schmalz and the captain finally realised their mistake, it was too late. The Medusa ran aground and got stuck in the sand – several miles from the coast.

Crew and passengers now had to put their faith in the Medusa's lifeboats. But there weren't nearly enough of them. In order to save everyone, they set to crafting an extra lifeboat from wood ripped from the frigate, in the form of a raft of twenty by sixty-five feet. Three days after the ship ran aground, the raft was almost finished. Then, a storm rose. The hull of the Medusa groaned and the people aboard her feared she would break open. Panic spread on board. The captain decided to evacuate the ship immediately. 147 people clambered aboard the homemade raft. The other passengers climbed into the regular lifeboats. The plan was to have one of the lifeboats tow the raft. Unfortunately, this worked poorly. After a few brave attempts, the captain therefore made another, fateful decision: he cut the towlines. The lifeboats then made their way to the coast. The raft, abandoned and lacking rudder, oars and sail, was cast adrift. For the next thirteen days, it drifted this way and that on the open sea.

The death scenes in Ann Radcliffe's and Mary Shelley's novels, written around the same time, pale in comparison to the horrors that took place on board the raft during those thirteen days. Many of the passengers died during that first, stormy night after falling overboard or being crushed between the boards. The next morning, the sea had calmed, but instead they had to contend with the tropical sun; several people collapsed with sunstroke. Others suffered fever hallucinations. Three men committed suicide by throwing themselves into the sea. Wild fistfights broke out among the rest; sixty people were killed and, as if that weren't enough, virtually all their provisions were destroyed. The next day, the living began to eat the dead.

Shortly thereafter, new violence broke out, with more deaths as a result. Five days after the raft had been cut loose, thirty desperate men – and one woman – were still alive. Their hope of survival rested on their stores of human meat and a few crates of French wine – and the hope that their raft would be spotted by a passing ship. But no sails appeared on the horizon. On the seventh day, a handful of the remaining men, mainly officers, came up with a diabolical plan. They were going to get rid of the weakest members of the group in order to make the wine last longer. The ship's doctor, who had assumed the role of the raft's informal captain, made a list of twelve people that were to be sacrificed, among them the only woman and her husband. The soldiers loaded their rifles and executed the twelve. The weapons were then thrown overboard to, if possible, avoid any more bloodshed. It worked. The fifteen people who were still on the raft after that last massacre survived long enough to be picked up by a French brig, two weeks after the Medusa ran aground.

In Western Europe, shipwrecks had been fashionable for almost a century. You could read about them almost daily in newspapers and magazines: in France there was even a *Journal des naufrages* (*Journal of Shipwrecks*). They were the subject of detailed and passionate discussion in social circles. Many historical tragedies lingered in the collective consciousness: the mere mention of the names of lost ships such as the Saint Géran, the Britannia or the Minotaur – not to mention the Medusa – was enough to make people shudder. And it goes without saying shipwrecks found their way into the art and literature of the era. J. M. W. Turner, for instance, was powerfully affected by the cruel fate of the Minotaur – 570 people died when this British warship, on its way from Gothenburg to England, ran aground off the Dutch island of Texel in 1810 – and the Medusa's raft was immortalised in a famous painting by Théodore Géricault. The sinking of the Medusa also inspired one of the songs in Lord Byron's *Don Juan*.

On the literary side, the most popular narratives were the ones in which the shipwrecked himself (it was almost always

a man), told the story of how the ship he had been travelling aboard had foundered, how he had miraculously survived and how he had finally, preferably after a long absence, been able to return home. The most classic example of this genre is, of course, *Robinson Crusoe* (1719). But the shipwreck theme had many variations, and from the latter part of the eighteenth century, which is to say when Europeans were inventing modern beach life, the Robinsonades found unexpected competition. An alternative perspective evolved, characterised by a narrator who was no longer at sea, as tradition has dictated since the wanderings of Odysseus and the apostle Paul's shipwreck on Malta. Instead, he is safe on the shore, witnessing disaster. He looks on as a ship in distress drifts toward the coast. He watches the crew fight to avoid dangerous sand banks and rocks. From his safe vantage point, he imagines the situation on board, listens to the terrified cries of the passengers, sees them desperately throw themselves into the churning water – only to drown or be hurled against the rocks. He's horrified – but also strangely exhilarated – by his experience: by the sea and its pitiless violence.

A typical example of this genre is the shipwreck in Charles Maturin's novel *Melmoth the Wanderer* (1820). It takes place on Ireland's Atlantic coast, to which the young John Melmoth arrives in the wake of a rich uncle's death. When a storm blows in one night, Melmoth finds himself unable to sleep. He paces back and forth in his chamber, listening to the howling wind and the creaking and groaning of the house. In the end, he decides to get dressed and go down to the kitchen, where he finds all the servants gathered. They pray for everyone caught out at sea. Then, a canon shot rings out in the night! Everyone knows what that means: a ship in distress is calling for help. The men of the house ready themselves and head out into the storm. They struggle through the gale-force gusts. Somewhere out on the ocean, which is engulfed in darkness, they can hear desperate screaming. The men on the beach shout back. Waves crash over them. The foam sparkles in the night.

> Melmoth caught a full view of the vessel, and of her danger. She lay beating against a rock, over which the breakers dashed their foam to the height of thirty feet. She was half in the water, a mere hulk, her rigging torn to shreds, her main mast cut away, and every sea she shipped, Melmoth could hear distinctly the dying cries of those who were swept away, or perhaps of those whose mind and body, alike exhausted, relaxed their benumbed hold of hope and life together, knew that the next shriek that was uttered must be their own and their last. There is something so very horrible in the sight of human beings perishing so near us, that we feel one firm step rightly planted, one arm steadily held out, might save at least one, yet feel we know not where to fix that step, and cannot stretch that arm, that Melmoth's senses reeled under the shock, and for a moment he echoed the storm with yells of actual insanity. By this time the country, having been alarmed by the news of a vessel going to pieces on the shore, had poured down in multitudes; and those who, from experience or confidence, or even ignorance, repeated incessantly, "it is impossible to save her – every soul on board must perish," involuntarily quickened their steps as they uttered the words, as if they

were anxious to behold the fulfilment of their own prediction, while they appeared hurrying to avert it.

Melmoth watches one of the men go down to the beach in a heroic attempt to save one of the shipwrecked – only to be swept out to sea himself and perish. Everyone realises any attempt to come to the rescue is futile. And yet, they stay on the beach, shouting encouragement to the people fighting for their lives in the dark. Everyone pities them – but no one can avert their doom.

Mary Shelley, the horror novelist, penned a similar shipwreck scene in her short story *Transformation* (1831). The main character is Guido, an emotional young aristocrat from Genoa who loses everything he owns and, what's worse, the woman he loves. He leaves the city behind and wanders along the seashore. A storm is rising. Dark clouds appear from nowhere. The waves throw up their white crests and thunder crashes above the raging sea. Then, Guido suddenly spots a ship:

> In vain the mariners tried to force a path for her to the open sea – the gale drove her on the rocks. It will perish! – All on board will perish! – ... It was an awful sight to behold that vessel struggling with her fate. Hardly could I discern the sailors, but I heard them. It was soon all over! – A rock, just covered by the tossing waves, and so unperceived, lay in wait for its prey. A crash of thunder broke over my head at the moment that, with a frightful shock, the skiff dashed upon her unseen enemy. In a brief space of time she went to pieces.

There I stood in safety; and there were my fellow-creatures, battling, how hopelessly, with annihilation. Methought I saw them struggling – too truly did I hear their shrieks, conquering the barking surges in their shrill agony. The dark breakers threw hither and thither the fragments of the wreck: soon it disappeared.

The shipwreck in French author Bernardin de Saint-Pierre's *Paul & Virginia* (1788) is a classic variation on the same theme. It takes place on Mauritius. Young Paul is waiting for his fair Virginia to return to the island after an extended stay in France. His heart overflows with joy when he's told she's on her way, because when she returns, so it has been agreed, they will be married. But when he finally sights the ship she's on, dark clouds suddenly appear on the horizon. A tropical hurricane engulfs the island! The ship is unable to enter the harbour. Instead, it seeks shelter in a cove on the northern coast of the island, where it spends the next few hours fighting its fate. Paul sets out to find it. He makes it down to the beach where the locals have already gathered to watch the frigate's struggle against the elements. The sky is black. The seabirds are circling the ship, screeching as though entranced. Crew and passengers are on deck, their faces ashen. Paul spots Virginia and throws himself into the surf. Desperately, he tries to swim out to his beloved, but the waves hurl him back to shore. Massive breakers crash over the sides of the doomed ship. On the beach, shingles are flung fifty feet inland. And finally, the unthinkable happens: the ship is pushed onto rocks and her hull breaks.

The next morning, the narrator finds Virginia's young corpse on the beach.

She was half-covered with sand, her head and limbs in the position in which we had seen her perish. Her features had not visibly altered. Her eyes were closed and her face was still serene; but on her cheeks the pale violets of death mingled with the roses of modesty. One of her hand was on her clothes; the other, pressed against her heart, was tightly closed and stiffened. I opened it with difficulty and took from its grasp a little box; but what was my surprise when I saw that it was Paul's portrait, which she had promised him never to part with while she lived.

I am oddly moved by Saint-Pierre's book, can feel myself tearing up a little when I read the last few lines. I suppose it's the

fine detail, the realism used to evoke the destroyed ship and innocent Virginia's death. I try to imagine having to endure it: standing there on the beach, in the hurricane, watching M. vanish in the churning sea. Certainty dawning on me: I can't save her, her doom is final and irrevocable. The raging waves continue to crash against the shore, their roar mingling my own despairing scream of love. Under me I can hear the clattering of shingles and seashells, feel the sand and seaweed bury my toes. A sickening taste of salt in my mouth, seawater mixed with my tears. My own heart that keeps beating when someone else's has just stopped.

Two hundred years ago, such experiences were commonplace – and not just in literature. Thousands of people died every year in shipwrecks like the ones Maturin, Shelley and Saint-Pierre spun their yarns around. In seafaring nations like England, France, the Netherlands and Sweden, few families were spared; practically everyone had at least one relative who had met their fate at sea. World trade and travel flourished around the turn of the nineteenth century. Sea traffic exploded, but sea safety was virtually non-existent and the number of fatal accidents increased at an alarming rate. The majority occurred along coasts; the number of shipwrecks on the open sea was negligible in comparison. No less than 350 shipwrecks a year – almost one a day – were recorded on just the English side of the English Channel. Every year, an average of 5,000 Englishmen died in these shipwrecks. The situation was comparable on the French side.

But it wasn't just shipwrecks that became more common. The number of onlookers grew, too. In earlier times, many parts of the coast had been more or less uninhabited and the death struggle of a ship had rarely been witnessed by any sizable crowd; now, by contrast, the coasts were dotted with fashionable resorts where the wealthy spent large parts of the year. More than once, dinners, balls and concerts were interrupted by news that some ship or other had foundered. The guests would then eagerly head out to watch the spectacle. Or they lingered in one of the cafés lining the promenade, from where they could observe the catastrophe in real time through their opera glasses. The people on board were pitied. But many also found the experience thrilling. The seaside hotels were well aware of this and exploited it unabashedly in their marketing; from the early nineteenth century, the death of sailors on the beaches counted as one of the main attractions of the seaside resorts.

Perhaps it's no wonder shipwrecks became the go-to metaphor for the political, economic and social tumult of that era. The French Revolution in particular was often described as a storm at sea, in which the old regime's hopelessly outdated ship had foundered. During the subsequent Revolutionary and Napoleonic wars, the storm spread to neighbouring countries, and the entire European ship was torn to pieces. A lot of people died in this disaster. Others made it through by clinging to pieces of flotsam. And then there were those who watched the violent upheaval as if from the outside, much like in Maturin's and Saint-Pierre's novels: they stood on the beach and watched the tragedy unfold. Johann Wolfgang von Goethe belonged to this latter group; his passivity during the German mobilisation against Napoleon in 1806 disappointed a lot of people around him. Goethe preferred safety. "Rather like a man who looks down from a solid cliff onto the raging sea and cannot help the shipwrecked men below but also cannot be reached by the breakers ... Thus I stood there, safe and sound, and let the furious tumult pass by me." Hegel, the philosopher, expressed himself in similar terms when he, around the same time, formulated his view of the world and history. History, Hegel writes, is an appalling drama. Dreadful is the sight of all the evil in the world, of goodhearted people foundering, of grand states collapsing – yes, all these things fill us with sorrow. The Good Spirit within us wants to revolt, and it is with difficulty we endure the painful realisation that we cannot save those lost on the sea of history. In the end, we turn away. We escape into our individual, selfish lives. Or, put more succinctly: we stand on "the calmer shore and, from a secure position, smugly look on at the distant spectacle of confusion and wreckage".

But times were changing. The year 1815 marked the beginning of a new, more peaceful period in European history. And as far as shipwrecks were concerned, the Medusa Disaster provided a turning point. The horrifying tragedy caused a public outcry. In the autumn of 1817, when the case was heard by the French courts, it was all Parisians could talk about. The newspapers were filled with an endless stream of witness testimonies and reports about the gruesome raft drama. The exceptional circumstances were the last drop: nothing that terrible could ever be allowed to happen again! France's new king Louis XVIII provided funds for and approved a project that would remedy the dangers of sea travel once and for all. The project centred on a thorough modernisation of the nation's lighthouses. The fundamental principle was that every ship that sailed along the French coast should always be within sight of a lighthouse. That way, captains would have an easier time determining their position – and thus avoiding the kind of mistake the Medusa had paid for so dearly.

France's lighthouses were to be upgraded with a new type of powerful lens, developed by the ingenious physicist Augustin Fresnel. First in line was a historic lighthouse: Cordouan, located on a desolate rock where the Gironde River spills out into the Atlantic. It had originally been erected in the sixteenth century on the initiative of none other than Michel de Montaigne, the famous essayist who at the time also happened to be the mayor of nearby Bordeaux. The Cordouan lighthouse was colloquially known as the "Versailles of the Sea", but its

proud, palatial appearance provided little assistance to nocturnal navigators; over the years, a large number of ships had sunk in the area, despite the lighthouse. The impact of the new Fresnel lens was immediate. Sailors praised the new technology. The king was pleased, too, for what could better symbolise a modern and enlightened monarchy than a powerful lighthouse, which used scientific insights about the nature of light to, quite literally, enlighten the night, tame the sea, facilitate trade and save human lives?

The rest of Europe soon followed France's example. Sweden-Norway became the first country outside of France to order a Fresnel lens, followed by the Netherlands. The British were more reluctant; it stung to admit the superiority of the French system. After fierce debate, lighthouse engineer Alan Stevenson eventually managed to convince the Royal Northern Lighthouse Board in Scotland to invest in Fresnel lenses. Thomas Stevenson, Alan's younger brother, also helped equip the Scottish coast with French-style lighthouses. His son, Robert Louis, on the other hand, disappointed his father by breaking with family tradition and choosing a career as a writer – to the benefit of those of us who have enjoyed stories like *Dr. Jekyll & Mr. Hyde* and *Treasure Island*. In the latter, the protagonists eventually find their gold. The narrator, however, aptly recalls the sacrifices and sufferings of the Hispaniola's crew that have led them to their goal:

"That was Flint's treasure that we had come so far to seek, and that had cost already the lives of seventeen men from the Hispaniola. How many it had cost in the amassing, what blood and sorrow, what good ships scuttled on the deep, what brave men walking the plank blindfold, what shot of cannon, what shame and lies and cruelty, perhaps no man alive could tell."

4

Engulfed

I can't remember passing any lighthouses when, many summers ago, I wandered along the beautiful beaches of Costa Rica's Pacific coast. There must have been lighthouses around somewhere because I wasn't far from Puntarenas, one of Central America's most important ports, and the reefs off the coast are infamously treacherous. And yet, although I was often out after dark, I never noticed any nocturnal pulses of light. Their absence amplified the illusion of the unspoiled natural state of the tropical coastal landscape. I rarely saw another soul. At times, I was overcome with a bizarre conviction I was the first human ever to walk that beach.

But then one evening, I had company. I had decided to spend the night on the beach and had set up camp near some

red boulders above the tidal zone. Just as I was about to fall asleep, my ear caught the sound of voices. In the moonlight, I could see two human forms. It was almost midnight and their arrival surprised me because there were no roads to the remote stretch of beach I had sought out. I watched the two from afar as they unhurriedly strolled down to the water's edge. Once there, they sat down on a rock, seemingly unaware of my presence. They remained there for a long time, talking quietly with their eyes on the horizon, contemplating something, I know not what. Life, death, human existence. At least that's how I imagine it. But when they finally stood up to, as I assumed, turn back inland, to return to wherever they belonged, I realised with some surprise they were in fact undressing. Then they took each other's hands and waded out into the sea. The waves broke over their moonlit bodies. When they got further out, they began to swim, with slow, dreamlike strokes. They moved farther and farther from the shore. Eventually, their bobbing heads disappeared from view. I stayed where I was and gazed out at the sea, waiting for them to return. I must have sat there for close to an hour. I waited and waited – but in vain.

The next day, I soon had other things to worry about as I tripped on a sharp rock and severely injured my foot, which forced me to seek medical attention. I didn't think about my nocturnal experience again until a week later, on my way back to Europe. At the Panama City airport, I came across a book with a peculiar title: *Columbina's Kiss*. It was a novel. The author was a young Brazilian woman, Adriana Lisboa. I suppose it was the cover that caught my eye, because it was a picture of a seashore. On the beach stood a young man in blue shorts, his gaze fixed on the unbroken horizon. I bought the book and read it from cover to cover on the overnight flight to Amsterdam.

The book is set in Mangaratiba outside Rio de Janeiro, where a young author by the name of Teresa lives with her boyfriend, the unassuming Latin teacher João. The Atlantic roars outside their windows. Teresa's life seems to be on the cusp of dramatic change. She has just had her big break as an author. Her most recent novel has won several awards. A glossy magazine has come by to do an at-home article about her. She watches in astonishment as sales of her books skyrocket. She no longer has to tutor students in Portuguese. But something is bothering her. She has just turned 35, an age that in the context of literary awards marks the boundary between young and old authors. The age Dante was, I thought to myself, when he found his way into Hell.

João worries about her, but even though they've lived together for six months, he finds it difficult to get close to her. He wants to "get to the bottom of Teresa, to the heart of the labyrinth of her soul, that centre point where a haiku by Bashō is written in the sand". But he's unable.

He's afraid she will leave him.

Every evening, before sunset, the two of them go down to the beach for a swim. Teresa is an excellent swimmer and heads out into the bay. João, on the other hand, takes no "unnecessary risks", even though the sea is calm. He dives under water a few times and takes "a few cautious Latin teacher strokes". Then he returns to shore, sits down in the sand and watches the woman he loves swim.

But one day, Teresa goes down to the beach without João. She wades out into the water and swims away, further and further, until she's nothing but a tiny dot on the horizon. Then she disappears. When darkness falls, João takes a seat on the veranda of their house. He sits there under a star-strewn sky, waiting for Teresa to return. But just like the two people I saw on the beach in Costa Rica, she doesn't.

What happened? João speculates about a possible asthma attack, that Teresa might have been eaten by a shark or kidnapped by pirates. Or that maybe there never was a Teresa, maybe he imagined their relationship, their love. The journalists that force their way into their house have their own theories. Teresa has put up a poem on the refrigerator door, a stanza by Manuel Bandeira:

> In the waves of the beach
> in the waves on the sea
> I want to be happy
> I want to drown.

They exchange significant looks. So, suicide?

I put the book down. What time was it anyway? A meaningless question since I was travelling through time zones. Exhaustion weighed on my eyelids. I leaned back in my seat and closed my eyes. I thought about the vast Atlantic, the churning blackness, glistening in the starlight, billowing far below.

Lisboa's novel brought to mind a French film I'd seen a year or two earlier, François Ozon's *Under the Sand*. It's a story

What is it that makes a person want to become one with a dark ocean? Where does our desire to be engulfed come from?

From the Romantic era, of course. From the *early* Romantic era, around the turn of the nineteenth century. By then, beach life was fashionable in Europe; England's coasts in particular were lined with chic seaside resorts. But the Romantics saw something in the ocean that the sea bathers of the eighteenth century had failed to notice: they saw themselves in the briny depths. They made the seashore a laboratory for exploring the self. There, they felt, they could get closer to the human soul than anywhere else. "I love the sea like my soul," Heinrich Heine confides in his diary in 1826. "Often, it even seems to me that the sea really is my soul." From the fishermen in Norderney, where he often walked along the beach in the evenings, he had heard tell of sunken cities where church bells still rang every Sunday. In the same way, he pondered, every person contains a mysterious, sunken world. That idea eventually came to form the basis of not just innovative poetry and philosophy, but also of modern psychoanalysis.

Caspar David Friedrich's paintings convey the relationship between the sea and the human soul with eerie precision. The open sea sparkles in the moonlight, secretive, silvery and opaque. The people on shore are imbibing a nature that is magical and alive, fantasising about what might lie hidden beyond the horizon and down in the black abyss. But more than anything they're busy exploring – and interrogating – themselves. There goes the lonely monk, wandering across the dunes, filled with anxiety, doubting his God, his faith, with his eyes fixed on the vast ocean. There are the young friends, standing up on the chalk cliff that drops precipitously toward the beach below, pondering the miracle and fragility of life. And from the rocky shore, the old men and women watch the ships approach out of the dusk – and contemplate the passing of their own lives. They see how they themselves will, like the distant ships, one day reach their final port of call.

The Romantics saw in the ocean a force of nature that like themselves resisted reason and humanity's need to force logical order upon the world, resisted science's claims of being able to explain the inexplicable. The sea urged the Romantics to abandon their rational selves and instead plumb the depths of their souls, their inner ocean – their subconscious, as Freud would later put it – for that part of our nature that has been lost to civilisation. With their backs to the organised, civilised world and their eyes on the primitive, unruly waves that refused to be tamed, they gave in to the temptation to dive – literally and figuratively – into a deeper, truer and more fertile region, out of reach of the barren tentacles of reason. Down there, the Romantics, threatened as they felt by the impending machine age, of a mechanical worldview, found a refuge. There, they could once again become who they really were.

Getting lost in the depths, letting yourself be swallowed up, wanting to drown – what it meant was finding a way back to yourself.

The Romantics, overcome with Thanatos, wanted to drown, and some of them, like Shelley, did. Carl Gustav Jung, the romantically inspired psychoanalyst, almost met the same fate in his youth. The Romantics dreamed of setting sail, on the sea, in life – and capsizing halfway, foundering in an (emotional) tempest, was reaching your destination. The ideal (life) achievement – from Novalis' *Heinrich von Ofterdingen* (1802) to Schubert's last symphony – was the unfinished work. And as they wandered along the beaches, over seaweed and empty seashells, they felt the ocean calling. They willingly gave in to the hypnotic monotony of its rhythm. They longed to get down there, to the netherworld they could only ever access through their dreams. They could feel the falling, the sinking inside.

I must have drifted off, because when I opened my eyes the cabin was flooded with light. The morning sun, rising in the east, poured in through the small windows. I looked out and saw that my journey high above the nocturnal ocean was coming to an end. Tiny clouds hung above the North Sea coast. Central America, which I had left in the west, now existed only in my memories. As though my time there belonged to a previous life.

German ethnologist Leo Frobenius coined the term *Nachtmeerfahrt* – "night-sea journey". There are hardly any cultures, he writes in *The Age of the Sun God* (1904), that haven't asked themselves where the sun goes at night, after disappearing into the sea in the evening. Isn't it a miracle that it reappears every morning – and not in the west, where it vanished, but in the east? As long as there have been humans on Earth, they have tried to interpret this resurrection. They have spun legends and myths about gods and humans who, like the sun, disappear into the night-sea – and who travel through it, underneath the surface. Frobenius called these narratives "whale myths", after the Biblical story of Jonah.

SCHEMATISCHE DARSTELLUNG DER WALFISCHMYTHE.

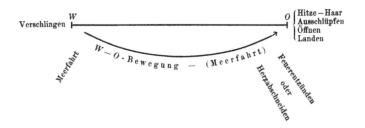

Carl Gustav Jung reinterpreted the night-sea journey in psychological terms: to be swallowed by a whale was to experience a personal crisis, and the journey across the night-sea was the road to the rebirth of the soul. In this sense, many of us have, at one time or another, travelled through the belly of the beast, through murky waters, on our way to the opposite shore: on our way toward something new, a new life stage.

In *Sous le sable*, Marie is eventually contacted by the Landes police. "We have recovered a body from the sea that fits your husband's description." She's asked to travel down to identify the body. She's reluctant. Because she doesn't really want it confirmed. She wants to hold onto the possibility: That it never happened.

As it turns out, Jean had been taking anti-depressants for a while. The news comes as a shock to Marie because Jean never indicated to her that he was unhappy. His mother, on the other hand, isn't surprised; when Marie visits her at the nursing home where she lives, she says she knows her son was suffering:

> But I don't for a second believe Jean killed himself, or even drowned. The truth is crueller: He disappeared simply because he was bored. Or, to be more precise: because he was bored of *you*. He wanted a new life. Start over. You can understand that, can't you? Many men dream of doing that.

Marie returns to the Atlantic shore in the final scene. Autumn has come. No one's swimming. Sand blankets the seaweed and driftwood. Marie digs her fingers into it. She listens to the waves and cries a little. But then, as she turns her head, she notices a large man standing at the water's edge. He stands there with his hands on his hips, watching the crests of the waves sparkle in the sun. "It's Jean!" she thinks to herself, and her face fills with joy. She stands up – and runs to him.

In *Um beijo de Colombina*, João believes Teresa drowned. He ponders the Bandeira poem that still hangs on the fridge, the one that seems to exult in death. But there's a twist in the story when João one day spots the supposedly dead woman in town, alive and in the company of a new life partner.

She has been reborn.

It's been a few years since that summer now. As I write this, I once again find myself on a tropical coast. Night has fallen. I'm tossing and turning in a cheap hotel room. The monkeys are asleep in the trees. Through the screened window I can hear the rumbling of the ocean. I slip on my sandals and step outside, stroll down through the rainforest, down to the beach. It's deserted. The ghost crabs scuttle across the sand. The waves gleam in the moonlight, as though the ocean were made of metal.

"WARNING! RIP CURRENTS!"

exclaims a rusty sign sitting next to a palm tree.

I undress and wade out into the salty, warm water. It's completely opaque, but it cools my sweaty body. The shingles clack as the waves advance and retreat. I wade further out. Keep walking until I can't reach the bottom. Then I swim a few strokes and set my sights on the horizon.

5

Katabasis

In Cartagena, Luis says, the beach is grey at dawn. He points to the barrel of his G3 when he says this, *steel grey*, he says. He smiles. The sand is white, he says, this colour, tapping his teeth. And when the sun comes up on your right, man, it is a slow-motion explosion like in the movies, a big kerosene flash and then the water is sparkling grey and orange and red. Luis is full of shit, of course, but he can talk and it is true that he is the only one of our *gallada* who has seen the Caribbean. Who has been to Cartagena.

My companion and I sat quietly next to each other and let the hum of the car engine accompany the male narrator's half reassuring, half distraught voice. Nam Le's short stories were the best I'd heard in a long time – and the audiobook format suited them perfectly. I listened to the words that kept flowing out of the speakers, imbibed them – and at the same time I contemplated the weeks we had spent together, M. and me. A long, hot summer on the continent – in Berlin, Munich, Vienna and Geneva – for work, as it were. But now we had left Berlin behind and were travelling north. We were headed for the Baltic coast, via the treelined roads of Brandenburg. And I felt a thrill of anticipation at the prospect of seeing the sea again.

From time to time, we stopped to explore some part of former East Germany with its sleepy villages and beautiful lakes. We passed Gransee, Großwoltersdorf and Stechlin. In Rheinsberg we swam in the lovely Grienericksee. Shortly thereafter, we arrived in a to-me-unknown town by the name of Mirow. As we drove through it, a soaring steeple with a baroque spire caught our eye as it rose from a copse of ancient oak trees. For a modest fee, we were able to climb the tower. On our way, we made a strange discovery: halfway up, one of the floors held a dozen bookcases. It turned out the town's public library had felt a need to cull a large number of its books, and for lack of a better place to store them, the books had been moved to the church. Now, they were offered for sale, for the attractive price of one euro per book. We stared at the collection in wonder – and then started to browse. This is how I acquired several books that day, of which I grew attached to one in particular: a beautiful old copy of Rainer Maria Rilke's *The Notebooks of Malte Laurids Brigge*. A onetime borrower had scribbled something on the inside of the dark-yellow cover and the Insel Verlag logo – a two-masted ship – looked a bit worn, but other than that the book was in excellent condition. Printed in 1926, the title page informed me. The year Rilke died.

Knowing it was a famous book, I opened it immediately and started reading. The notebooks began with what looked like a diary entry, jotted down on 11 September – of all days – on Rue Toullier in Paris. "*So, also hierher kommen die Leute, um zu leben*", I read, pronouncing the words under my breath, "*ich würde eher meinen, es stürbe sich hier.*" I glanced over at

M., who seemed absorbed in an East German copy of Japanese author Kobo Abe's *The Woman in the Dunes*.

Afterwards, we sat for a while in the park by the church. We ate our packed lunches and looked through our newly purchased books. I read about Malte, who had just moved to Paris, with nothing but a suit, his writing implements and a trunk full of books. He aspires to be a writer. But life in the metropolis changes him, alters his character, turns his worldview upside down. He's horrified by how "a completely different perception of all things has formed in me". Memories from his childhood, from his previous life, cause additional confusion. He continues to write. He writes about the incredible, the upsetting, the horrifying – "das Entsetzliche" as he puts it, or "das Unheimliche" as Freud would later call it.

What he really wants to write is poetry. But he hesitates, doubts his ability. Because

> poems written early in life don't amount to much. One should wait and gather meaning and sweetness a whole life long – and as long a life as possible – then, at the very end, one might possibly write ten lines that are any good. For poems aren't, as people think, feelings (one has those early enough); they're experiences. To write a single line of verse one must see many cities, people, things, one must know animals, one must feel birds flying and know the movements flowers make as they open up in the morning. One must be able to think back to roads in unfamiliar regions, unexpected encounters, and partings which one saw coming long before; one must be able to think back to those days in one's childhood that

are still unexplained, to one's parents whom one could not help offending when they brought a delightful gift and one didn't appreciate it (it was a delight for someone else), to those childhood illnesses which arose so peculiarly and with so many profound and difficult changes, to those days in peaceful and secluded rooms, and to those mornings by the sea, to the sea anywhere...

And then, he is seized by a sudden notion: "At some point might it be possible," he writes, "to go see the sea?"

If Malte Laurids Brigge's sudden *Drang zum Meer* was an expression of Rilke's own longing for the sea, it was about to be fully satisfied. In October 1911, shortly after he finished *Malte*, the then-thirty-five-year-old Rilke was invited by Duchess Marie von Thurn und Taxis-Hohenlohe to visit Castle Duino, dramatically situated atop a cliff by the Adriatic Sea. His stay there would play a pivotal role in his authorship. The poet was fascinated by the evocative castle, which, from the coast between Trieste and Venice, looked out at the "most open sea-space". All his life, he'd been searching for places like this; places with a Romantic atmosphere that could provide deep inspiration and give rise to great feats of poesy. And he was in dire need of such inspiration, because since *Malte*, he'd begun to sense an alarming emptiness inside himself, an impending poetic drought.

Just after New Year's in 1912, it seemed his high expectations of Duino were justified. Inspiration welled up inside him. First, he finished the short poetic cycle *Das Marien-Leben*.

Then came the true breakthrough, in the form of an episode that is well known to literary historians today and was thoroughly – one is tempted to say: too thoroughly – recounted by his hostess at the castle at the time:

> One morning he received an annoying business-letter; he wanted to deal with it at once, and was forced to immerse himself in figures and prosaic matters. A violent bora, as we call the north wind in those parts, was blowing, but the sun was shining and the sea was radiantly blue, crested with silver. Rilke went down to the bastions that jut out to east and west and are connected by a narrow path at the foot of the castle. From there the rocks drop down steeply to the sea, which lies two hundred feet below. He was walking up and down immersed in thought, for the answer he had to write to the business-letter preoccupied him. All of a sudden, in the middle of his cogitations, he stopped still, for it seemed to him that he heard a voice call through the roaring of the wind:
>
> 'Who, if I cried out, would hear me among the angelic orders?'
>
> He stood motionless and listened. 'What was that?' he whispered, 'what is coming?'
>
> He took the notebook he always carried and wrote down these words, as well as a few more lines that had formed themselves without any conscious effort on his part. Who was coming? Now he knew: the god.
>
> Very calmly he went up to his room, laid the notebook away and wrote the business-letter. Yet by the same evening the whole of the First Elegy had been written down.

He felt a great relief – and wonder, too, because the elegies that grew inside him from this point on were markedly different from anything he had penned before. Indeed, they appeared intent on upending his fundamental understanding of what poetry was and had to be, and more than that: his entire world-view suddenly seemed in question. A new space of possibility opened up – like the endless, glittering sea-space in the south.

He continued to write, and a few more elegies took shape. Below the castle walls, the sea reflected the pale winter sun. Staccato waves heaved themselves ashore. In the morning, the fishermen continued their usual work, as though nothing had happened. Often, the unmistakable smell of salt and seaweed reached the castle.

To Rilke, however, the sea didn't only provide a source of poetic inspiration. It also made him feel anxious. "Neither the house nor the climate," he writes to Lou Andreas-Salomé that winter, appeals to him: "this constant shifting between bora and scirocco is not good for my nerves." He paces up and down the halls, along the sea-facing bastions, working on his new cycle of poems. But after a few weeks of intense work, that eerie sense of emptiness returns, that creative drought, that infertility.

One night, at a dinner party, he's told the unpleasant story of his countryman Ludwig Boltzmann's cruel fate. Boltzmann's career was very different from the poet's. He'd spent his life in laboratories and lecture halls, pondering equations and integrals; Rilke had lived the Romantic dream as a rootless poet. But on a deeper level, they were soulmates: both had dedicated their lives to a restless search for truth, absolute truth, absolute fundamentals: both wanted to get at the innermost heart of the universe, whether in the shape of angels or atoms, love or entropy – they had simply chosen different approaches, different strategies to get there.

And they both feared the creative drought.

Since the 1870s, Boltzmann had gone from strength to strength as a scientist and lecturer. Granted, his theories were the object of heated controversy, but at the end of the day, he'd made a name for himself within his field. These days, Boltzmann's elegant equations, especially in the area of thermodynamics, are required reading in physics classes the world over.

But around the turn of the nineteenth century, Boltzmann's health deteriorated. He experienced recurring bouts of depression. According to his doctors, he suffered from "neurasthenia", or, as we say nowadays, burn-out. At the same time, his asthma became more pronounced. In the spring of 1906, his condition was such he could no longer teach. He felt ill and miserable. Following

the advice of his friends, he decided to seek out a clinic for nervous conditions in Munich. But he couldn't bear it there; he returned to Vienna after just a few days. His wife Henriette then suggested the whole family might relocate to some peaceful place in the countryside. Boltzmann accepted. It was August by the time the family arrived on the Adriatic coast. They checked into the elegant Hotel Ples in Duino, near the castle.

But the salt and the damp, the sand and the rocks, the wind and the shrill screeching of the gulls did not have a palliative effect on Boltzmann. If anything, the holiday atmosphere in Duino plunged him deeper into melancholy. He felt nervous and anxious and soon insisted on returning to Vienna. His family tried to persuade him to stay, but to no avail. The day before his planned departure, on 5 September 1906, Boltzmann was deep in the doldrums. After breakfast, Henriette went to see him. She wanted to take his suit to the local cleaners. This led to an intense quarrel, because Boltzmann feared the cleaning of his suit would delay his departure. After the quarrel, his wife and the couple's youngest daughter, fifteen-year-old Elsa, went down to the beach for a swim. Boltzmann had mumbled something about joining them. But he never did. His wife and daughter waited in vain.

The waves lapped against the shore, a few children played at the water's edge, it was a lovely late-summer's day by the Adriatic. But there was no sign of Boltzmann. At length, Henriette asked her daughter to go find her father. She went back to the hotel and knocked on his door. No one opened. She tried the handle and the door opened. But when she stepped inside, she was met by a gruesome sight: Boltzmann's massive body hung lifeless from a sturdy curtain rod. He'd hanged himself.

Another unpleasant story Rilke became familiar with around this time was about an author. In this case, the main character was fictional, though some claimed to see a resemblance with famed composer Gustav Mahler, who had died in May of 1911. The story reached Rilke in the autumn of 1912 through two successive issues of the magazine *Neuer Rundschau*. It was called *Death in Venice*.

Rilke, who had a close relationship with Venice and its eccentricities (which would play a significant part in the *Duino Elegies*), felt ill at ease at reading his contemporary Thomas Mann's short story. The first few pages alone were enough to alarm him because Gustav von Aschenbach's "artist fear of not having done, of not being finished before the works ran down" was an eerie reflection of his own fear of the *Duino Elegies* remaining unfinished. Furthermore, he disliked the story as a whole. Aschenbach, who has taken up residence on the barrier island of Lido, allows himself to be lulled by the pleasant holiday atmosphere by the sea. There, he makes the acquaintance of the "perfectly beautiful" boy Tadzio. But as the summer draws to a close, he learns that a cholera epidemic is ravaging the city. Death, lurking in the stinking, sewer-like canals, suddenly insists on having his attention. At the same time, he's increasingly ensorcelled by the beautiful Tadzio. He increasingly loses himself in an abyss of emotion. He's driven to reject everything that previously seemed meaningful to him. He embraces chaos and revulsion. He has wild, obscene dreams. His soul has a taste of "the bestial degradation of his fall".

In the final scene, Gustav von Aschenbach is dying on the beach. He suffers "spells of giddiness only half physical in their nature, accompanied by a swiftly mounting dread, a sense of futility and hopelessness". Summer is over; the sea spreads out pale and autumnal before him. The sand is grey and dirty, the beach appears empty and deserted. Aschenbach is seated in a lounge chair with a blanket on his knees. Then he spots Tadzio. He watches as a playmate wrestles the beautiful boy into the sand. He almost wants to jump up and save the godlike creature. But Tadzio quickly frees himself and strolls toward the water's edge with his head bowed. He draws a picture in the sand with the tip of his toe and then wades out into the sea. When he turns around and meets Aschenbach's eyes, the dying man believes he can see the boy smile at him and wave. But in the next moment, his heart has stopped beating.

Rilke felt the story was about something that "is no longer told, it flows out and saturates everything, and one sees it growing larger and larger, like spilled ink". He took issue with the narrative style, which he claimed failed to give the reader anything firm to hold onto, with the lack of contours, and with all the "fumes, smells, turbidities that blend together". Ironically, much of this was reminiscent of Rilke's own expressionist style, as it manifests itself in *Malte*.

Rilke was unable to complete the *Duino Elegies* during his stay on the Adriatic Sea. Instead, he sank into a lengthy and severe creative crisis he was unable to overcome until a decade later in Switzerland. Over the course of just a few weeks there, he finished not just the *Duino Elegies* but also his *Sonets to Orpheus*. But he paid a high price. He fell ill with what was eventually diagnosed as a particularly painful – and incurable – type of leukaemia. On 29 December 1926, he passed away at Valmont Sanatorium outside Montreux. It had been fifteen years since god had revealed himself to him in Duino. The castle had changed beyond recognition in the intervening years. It had ended up on the frontline of the First World War and been badly damaged in the violent clashes history books call the "Battles of Isonzo". Duchess Marie von Thurn und Taxis had stood out on a balcony in Trieste, watching as her ancestral home atop its cliff on the other side of the bay met its fate.

My companion had taken over the wheel. As we continued north, we listened to more of Nam Le's short stories and I thought about Rilke and Malte Laurids Brigge, about Boltzmann and Gustav von Aschenbach. In due course, evening fell. A dark August night settled over Mecklenburg. Before

long, the surrounding landscape was shrouded in darkness. But an hour later, the smooth, sleep-inducing asphalt under us gave way to a potholed, dilapidated cobblestone street. A town rose up on either side of it. It was deserted. The car kept going for a while longer, bouncing across the cobbles. Then, it stopped. The narrator of Nam Le's stories was still in Colombia:

"So you are really going to Cartagena?" Claudia says.

"Yes."

"Why?"

"Why?" To myself I think, to see the ocean. But I say, "What did you want to talk to me about? I have important business tonight."

"What business?"

There is no reason not to tell her. I say, "I am meeting with my agent".

"So it is real," she says. "You have been summoned."

When I opened the car door, unmistakable sea air flooded in. It brought with it a familiar soughing sound: it was the Baltic Sea. We climbed out of the car and strolled off in the direction of the sound, toward a dark wall, which, framed by the surrounding buildings, presumably constituted the nocturnal sea. We found our way to a flight of concrete steps covered in weeds and littered with broken glass, which led down to the beach. The sound grew louder. Voices reached us from somewhere, excited teenage voices. It sounded like people playing volleyball, though I have no idea how that could be possible in the dark. A bit further down the beach, a slightly older group had made a fire. We could hear the clinking of beer bottles and quiet conversation. We trudged through the sand. My companion shivered slightly; I put my arm around her. After we rounded a point and the lights from the town were no longer visible, we sat down by the foot of a tall dune. I let M. in under my roomy summer jacket. We sat there in the sand, pressed against each other. We relished the brackish smell, the cool damp, the gentle murmur of the sea.

We had reached our destination.

6

Longing

Why does Gustav von Aschenbach go to Venice?

Because Death has caught his attention.

It happens on a spring day back in Munich. After a stroll in the English Garden, he's waiting for the tram. The stop is right next to the Northern Cemetery. There's something eerie about the place. Not another soul to be seen, no vehicles. While he waits, he studies the headstones lined up behind the stonecutter's fence. His eyes are then drawn to the byzantine edifice of the adjacent mortuary chapel. There, in the portico above the two apocalyptic beasts guarding the front steps, he spots the red-headed figure of a man with an ominous look about him. The man stares at Aschenbach. In that moment, he senses something changing within him. He "felt the most surprising consciousness of a widening of inward barriers, a kind of vaulting unrest". He chooses to interpret it as "a youthfully ardent thirst for distant scenes". And the scene he longs to seek out is the sea.

Gustav von Aschenbach isn't the only one to have experienced such a longing for the sea. Indeed, many have: people who, when they sensed their time was nigh, found their way to the sandy shores of whatever continent they were on to await the inevitable. It should preferably happen in late summer, in August or September. Why then? I assume it has to do with the mood of the season. With the fading sun, the sand that no longer burns your feet. With the sighing of the wind through trees, which now presages winter sleep, and with the timeless waves that continue to roll ashore. With all the things that tell us the world keeps turning, indifferent to our human plight.

On the morning of 2 July 1881, the president of the United States, James A. Garfield, was supposed to board a train in Washington. But when he arrived at the station, a stranger leapt out of the shadows, pulled out a revolver and fired two shots. Just sixteen years after the assassination of Abraham Lincoln, there had been another attempt on the life of the nation's leader.

One of the bullets grazed Garfield's arm. The other penetrated his stomach. Garfield collapsed on the cold concrete floor of the train station. "My God, what is this?" he exclaimed. He remained conscious, but the pain was tremendous, as was the shock. He was brought back to the White House. His personal physician and friend D. W. Bliss quickly came to his side, along with a number of medical experts. Their attempts to treat the gunshot wound, however, did more harm than good. The bullet was left inside Garfield's abdomen. A month after the attack, the president was still alive, but his condition was far from stable. The people watching over him were thrown from hope to despair and back again. Would he recover after all?

For a while longer, people held out hope. But by early August, Garfield was running a high temperature. Puss was observed around the wound in his abdomen and his doctors decided to perform a minor surgery. It was unsuccessful. Then it was concluded the President's digestive system was in poor shape. In just a week, Garfield's weight plummeted from a robust 210 pounds to 130. Desperation grew. The President realised his life was coming to an end.

The summer heat in the American capital was difficult to endure, the air oppressive and humid. Garfield's sickbed was regularly swarmed by mosquitoes from a nearby swamp. The situation grew increasingly intolerable. The president consulted himself, his wife, his doctors. There was no agreement on what to do next. But in the end, he was unable to hold back his dearest wish. A longing had taken root in him: to see the ocean one last time. To listen to the breaking waves and to "rest in the large silence of the sea air", as he himself put it. Like Gustav von Aschenbach, he experienced a kind of youthful thirst for distant scenes.

At first, his doctors shook their heads. They firmly opposed allowing a, as it now seemed, mortally wounded man like Garfield to undertake a journey to the coast. It was considered far too risky. But the patient insisted, pleaded and begged. What did he really have to lose? The doctors admitted they would not be able to save his life. In the end – the patient was after all the president – they acquiesced. In early September, a train was readied. Garfield was carried aboard on a stretcher, then they set off. The destination was the fashionable resort Elberon in New Jersey.

The sun was setting when the train arrived. The clouds scudding across the sky were blushing pink. There was a light breeze. Garfield could now hear the heavy breathing of the Atlantic. "Thank God," he exclaimed. "It is good to be here."

Journalists, family and several government officials checked into a nearby hotel. As they waited for the inevitable they enjoyed the New Jersey beach life. The children played in the sand. The death watch lasted two weeks. Garfield found comfort in seeing and hearing the sea from his bed. But Death stalked the beach impatiently. The people who were there found it hard to describe their emotional state, but they would never forget it, that late summer of waiting in Elberon. "To this day," Garfield's secretary Joe Stanley Brown wrote forty years later, "I cannot hear the sound of the low slow roll of the Atlantic on the shore, the sound which filled my ears as I walked from my cottage to his bedside, without recalling again that ghastly tragedy."

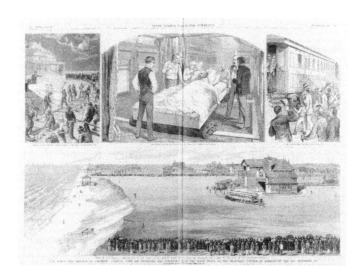

Just a few miles south of Elberon along the Jersey coast lies the affluent summer town of Bayhead Harbor, which provides the setting for Joyce Carol Oates' novel *A Fair Maiden*. The book chronicles the relationship between a teenage nanny, Katya Spivak, and financier, composer, artist and children's author Marcus Kidder, who is fifty years her senior. The latter has just entered remission after eighteen months of painful cancer treatments. He is worried about recurrence, and instead of waiting for the cancer to come back and enduring yet another, humiliating period of treatment, he decides to seize control of his own demise. He has a very clear idea of where and how it should happen: at his shore house, with the rumbling song of the Atlantic in the background and the air full of sun, salt and sand. But Marcus Kidder is less unassuming than Gustav von Aschenbach and James Garfield: for his seaside deathbed, he requires a fair maiden.

By now, it's the 2000s and beach life in New Jersey is very different from President Garfield's day. The shore houses of the wealthy jostle for space along the streets and Ocean Avenue is lined with luxury boutiques. Katya and Mr. Kidder first meet in front of a shop window. Katya is drawn to the charming, white-haired man's wealth, intelligence and debonair ways. Mr. Kidder's world couldn't be more different from her own working-class existence, which is dominated by her relationship with a criminal boyfriend, a less-than-affectionate mother and a father who has absconded after accumulating an unpayable amount of debt at the casinos of Atlantic City. She stares wide-eyed at Mr. Kidder's elegant house, which is remotely located near Bayhead's old lighthouse. The panorama window opens out onto views of the dunes, the sea, the unbroken horizon.

Marcus Kidder stares equally wide-eyed at Katya. She reminds him of the love of his youth, Naomi, whom he lost when she fell ill and died. He is inexorably drawn to Katya, feels that in her, he has found his fair maiden. Katya can sense that he desires her. She can also sense the presence of death but is unsure who the bell is tolling for. Not until late in the summer, when Mr. Kidder, during one of her many visits to his shore house, reads her a strange fairy tale, does she realise where things are going. The fairy tale is about a "kingdom by the sea". The king himself "was aged and longing to die" but needed a helping hand.

The night before Katya is due to leave Bayhead Harbor, it's time. Mr. Kidder's white limousine comes to pick her up. She makes no objection. She lets herself be brought to the shore house among the dunes one last time. A servant leads her up to the second floor, to a room with narrow windows and a stunning view of the sea. She undresses and gets into the bed. Mr. Kidder is already in it. The servant closes the blinds and lights some scented candles. Once they're alone, they drink champagne. Then Katya helps the old man swallow his pills. She kisses his forehead. They lie next to each other in silence for a while, listening to the waves that continue to roll in, to the wind that rustles through the beach grass. Just a few minutes later, Marcus Kidder is dead.

The main character in François Ozon's film *Time to Leave* is considerably younger. His name is Romain and he's only 31 when he finds out he has cancer – and only a five percent chance of survival. He rejects his doctors' attempts to treat his illness; like Marcus Kidder, he finds undergoing devastating radiation treatments and chemotherapy undignified. His decision means he has only three months to live. Romain considers how he wants to spend his last days and concludes that he wants to be alone. He breaks up with his partner and decides to travel to Brittany, to await the inevitable on the wind-lashed beaches of the Atlantic. When he gets there, he's pale and drawn. He wades out into the water, goes for a swim, gets back out and sits down in his lounge chair. The healthy, lively people around him enjoy the sunshine and the warm sand; it's the last golden days of the summer. But Romain is shivering. And yet, he stays on the beach until the sun sets. Dusk begins to fall and the screen gradually darkens. The waves continue to roll in for a while. Then the film is over.

It's already November. The bathing season is long since over. I take the *vaporetto* from St. Mark's Square to the Lido, gliding across the lagoon toward the elegant, mournful barrier island, without which Venice would have long since sunk into the Adriatic Sea. The smell of the lagoon's sweet, light-blue water wafts up to me where I stand by the railing; it mingles with the diesel fumes from the chugging boat engine. The tourists next to me have cameras slung around their necks, they're squinting not forward, in the direction of travel, but backward, toward the city that's now receding, as though it weren't real, but a mirage in the sea, about to dissolve. I watch as a young, Asian woman raises her arms as though to touch the wind. A little boy watches the boat's wake with delight. People sniff, look, listen.

I picture Gustav von Aschenbach's fateful arrival in Venice in Luchino Visconti's classic film adaptation, can almost hear the languorous adagietto from Mahler's fifth symphony, the mournful, momentous cadences of the harp. I watch the setting sun glint on the horizon, our life-giving star, whose light is broken only by the beautiful boy's silhouette. No offence to literature, I think to myself, but if there's an artform that better than any other is able to convey our longing to return to our origin, to die on the edge of the world – in this literal borderland between the firm and the fluid, between what moves and what doesn't – well, then that's probably film. Because this longing belongs to a world, I can feel it now, that won't let itself be written down – it's a sensuous longing, something we can see, hear, smell, but that, like a slippery fish, slithers out of our grasp if we try to hold onto it and understand it.

This time of year, the Lido's beach is virtually deserted. The lifeguards' tower is empty. Last summer's ice cream wrappers lie half-buried in the sand, fluttering in the wind. Out on the water, a giant oil tanker glides by, presumably on its way to the industrial port in Monfalcone, in the direction of Duino. I stroll along the water's edge and curiously wonder where on this beach Gustav von Aschenbach drew his last breath. Then I decide it doesn't matter; I remind myself Aschenbach is, after all, a fictional character, who, like Romain and Mr. Kidder, never actually existed.

I recall a piece in an American newspaper I once flipped through; in what context, I can no longer remember. It was about a middle-aged man from Los Angeles. After a sleepless night, he was said to have wandered through the still-sleeping city, down toward the sea, to Manhattan Beach. There, with the vast ocean in the west as his only witness, he shot himself dead. Why there? I remember asking myself back then. Why on the beach? The dead man had left his loved ones no explanation, no farewell note.

Gottfried Mücke, a well-known German businessman, died in the Maldives. At the age of eighty-two, he felt it was time. He headed to his dream beach, located on an island that is, and not for nothing, called Paradise Island. The morning after his arrival, he went down to the shore. He lay down in the sand, stretching out on his towel. One last time he allowed himself to enjoy the warmth of the sun, the gentle murmur of the waves, the muted voices of the people under nearby parasols. A smile curled his aged lips. Not until around lunchtime, at about twenty past twelve, did anyone realise his heart was no longer beating. "You couldn't wish for a more beautiful death," one of his loved ones commented – and someone added that beauty had always been Mücke's great passion: it was no coincidence he'd been a member of the Miss Germany jury several years in a row.

7

Terror

It's the second Sunday of Advent in Stockholm. The sun struggles to rise above the horizon. I flip through the thick Sunday paper over breakfast. One of the articles in this week's travel supplement is about the tropical islands of the Pacific, which two reporters decided to visit. They seem to have enjoyed themselves. Apparently, the trip was on the expensive side, but it was hardly wasted money. Because "on Aitutaki, one of the Cook Islands, they found paradise."

The Cook Islands? I pull out my phone, open Google Maps and search for the tiny archipelago. It turns out to be located in the middle of the South Pacific, just over a thousand miles northeast of New Zealand. I realise I know nothing about their history or culture, but I assume they were named in honour of James Cook, the British eighteenth century sea captain. I'm very familiar with Captain Cook; he was one of my idols growing up, particularly during my teenage years, when I dreamt of travelling the world and making sensational discoveries, in a Cookian manner. Cook was the most skilled of the European explorers when it came to mapping the unknown. His maps would play a pivotal role in shaping the future of the South

Pacific; they provided the basis for the West's interaction with – and colonisation of – this "invisible continent", as Le Clézio so aptly calls it.

For better or for worse, I might add.

> Swaying palm trees, turquoise seas and white sand combined with sun and balmy breezes do something special to our Nordic bodies and minds. [...] There's sunbathing, swimming, snorkelling, diving, sailing, paddling, stunningly beautiful nature experiences and a lot of time to just relax. The population is only about 2000 and we quickly slip into the locals' calm rhythm, far from any stress.

I suppose this is what we're looking for when we travel south: sun, heat, tranquillity. And we don't necessarily have to travel as far as the Cook Islands to have these needs met; the glossy travel magazines I sometimes sneak a peek in at the news stand are usually chockful of paradisical beaches and islands, located in every corner of our beautiful world, from Greece and Gambia to Mexico and Mauritius.

The beach is a realm of beauty, most paradisical of places. But "beauty", Rilke muses as he paces up and down the bastions of Duino, "is just the beginnings of terror". And in the tension between the two, our anxiety grows: the nagging worry about what could happen there, at the edge of the world. Who has not been overcome with the realisation at some point or another: that what we experience in our happiest moments is too wonderful, that it can't last forever, that the joy we're feeling in the moment means something horrifying is waiting around the corner, something bad enough to restore that great, sacred balance of the universe? "This calm is unnatural," thinks Tove Jansson's Fillyjonk as she washes her rug in the sparkling summer sea. "It means something terrible is about to happen."

The sun is setting, the early summer evening is perfect. Peals of laughter can be heard from a bonfire ringed by teenagers who are drinking beer, smoking weed, singing and having a good time. Chrissie is young and beautiful. A handsome young man catches her eye. Smiles are exchanged. She suddenly gets up and runs away. The young man follows. "Where are we going?" he asks. "Swimming!" she replies. They laugh and race across the dunes, shedding their clothes as they go. Cresting the last dune, the young man trips and tumbles down the slope to the beach. Chrissie is already halfway into the sea. The water's like a mirror, the unbroken horizon almost invisible in the twilight. The poor young man is far too intoxicated to get back on his feet and follow the bathing beauty; he remains slumped in the sand and falls asleep. But Chrissie swims out anyway, into the night. The warm water caresses her body, in the background she can still hear the reassuring sounds of the party. But then, suddenly: something sharp grabs her leg. She's pulled under. Her desperate screams echo through the summer night. Within seconds, she's gone. The next day, her badly mutilated corpse is found further up the beach. Crabs are voraciously chewing on what a few hours earlier was a happy young woman.

That's the opening scene of Steven Spielberg's 1975 horror classic, *Jaws*. During the days that follow, the animal claims further victims from the small seaside resort. Experts claim the bloodthirsty beast has been drawn to the beach by the happy shrieks and lively splashing of the beachgoers. The terrifying is drawn to the idyllic, is irked by it, wants to tear it apart.

In Peter Kihlgård's breakthrough novel *The Beach Man* the main character, who after a devastating divorce has decided to become a sand artist, decides to travel to Cuba. There, he gets to know Danish diplomat Poul, his wife Lene and their young son Love. One day, he accompanies Lene and Love to the old pirate town of Baracoa on the eastern tip of Cuba. On their way, they stop at a deserted and "blindingly white little beach lined with wild orange and beach almond trees" – in other words, a paradise beach. Lene immediately undresses and runs into the sea. The beach man makes sand patties with the child. He furtively studies Lene, her magnificent breasts, her slim waist and full hips. The boy is tired; Lene holds him and rocks him to sleep. She lays him down in his pram and parks it in the shade under an orange tree. The beach man and the beach woman are now alone. Their desire has awakened and the foreplay begins. The sea is sparkling, a breeze is blowing, the love juices are flowing. But then they hear an ominous, buzzing sound. The sun is darkened. What is casting the shadow? The man and woman roll over, she straddles him, grabs his member and is just about to insert it when the child suddenly screams, loudly, in panic and pain.

Terror has arrived.

I had never heard him scream like that before. We raced over to him. Now I could hear the buzzing, too. The high-pitched sound of thousands upon thousands of wild bees swarming, a cloud of bees around Love's pram. The child was screaming and coughing. Lene ran over, picked him up, howling, and raced toward the sea. I ran next to them and tried to swat bees off Love and Lene's bodies. The bugs did not pursue us. But it was too late. The child had been stung everywhere: his eyes, his nose, his throat – everything was swelling up. He turned blue. He wasn't screaming anymore. His little arms and legs twitched and then he was dead.

I am repulsed by it; nature's cruelty, its lack of mercy, the way it doesn't flinch at destroying us frail humans. Why does something like that have to happen? What's its purpose? Can't we just be allowed to stay there, in our paradise, without having to watch as our joy is turned inside out, as our dream morphs into a nightmare? What god wants this for us?

The holidaymakers who had travelled to the shores of the Indian Ocean for Christmas 2004 asked themselves the same thing. A quarter of a million people died on Boxing Day that year, in the great tsunami, the Biblical flood that inundated the coasts of Indonesia, Thailand, Sri Lanka and many other countries, obliterating everything in its path.

The South Pacific, too – home to the Cook Islands – have been hit by countless tsunamis over the centuries.

In Alex Garland's cult novel *The Beach*, death makes its entrances almost immediately. It speaks English with a Scottish accent, making the word "beach" sound like "bitch". And yet, the beach in question is a genuine paradise. It's located on a remote island in the Gulf of Thailand. The island is a nature preserve and trespassing is strictly forbidden. A group of young westerners defy the prohibition. They have secretly built a colony on the shores of the turquoise lagoon, among coral reefs and brightly coloured shoals of fish. They subsist on fishing, fruit picking and vegetable growing. The main character Richard quickly becomes a skilled spear fisher. Life seems easy, they work for a few hours in the morning and rest in the afternoon, swimming in the lagoon, socialising and smoking weed. On Sundays they play football in the tidal zone.

But their paradise is an unsustainable dream. Richard realises it can't last forever, that the colony he has found is doomed. He can sense something terrible awaits them all. On the one hand they fear their little beach community will, be discovered and dispersed. On the other, there's an internal threat, like in William Golding's *Lord of the Flies*, of simmering discontent and social tension. Informal cliques form. Fear creeps in. Collective food poisoning and a shark attack on three of the inhabitants signal that the end is nigh. But the ultimate trigger becomes the loss of the colony's boat – the beach community's only link to the outside world. Chaos and panic break out on the beach. Tempers flare and the different factions eventually clash in an armed battle. Richard decides to run away. In the dramatic final scene, he's chased by angry beach inhabitants who stab at him with knives and spears. Paradoxically, he enjoys it. Like Tove Jansson's disaster-loving Moomins, his innermost fear is that true horror will never rear its ugly head. When he thinks back on his time in paradise, it brings a smile to his face. He smugly touches the strange scars that remind him of the violence: "I carry a lot of scars. I like the way that sounds: I carry a lot of scars."

Terror, the Fillyjonk muses, is something "one can't ask anything of, nor argue with, nor understand, and that never tells one anything. Something that one can see drawing near, through a black window-pane, far away on the road, far away to sea, growing and growing but not really showing itself until too late." It grows in the calm, in uneventfulness. And suddenly, it explodes, seemingly out of nowhere, "having no cause and therefore requiring no explanation," as David Malouf puts it. It "gathers up into itself all kinds of hostilities". It induces anxiety. It begets violence, destruction and death.

When French-Algerian Mersault, in Camus' *The Stranger*, tries to explain to a court why he shot and killed a nameless "Arab" on a beautiful Mediterranean beach, he claims it was "because of the sun". And then he gives an account of what happened: how before the murder he experienced joy on the beach, how he swam in the turquoise water with his girlfriend and enjoyed lunch in the company of good friends. The world was good, terror kept at a safe distance. But then the sun climbed to its zenith and it was high noon. Blades of light shot up out of the sand, from bits of shell and broken glass. Mersault ambled along the water's edge, with the sound of lapping waves in the background and with the sun hammering down mercilessly from a cloudless sky. He balled his fists in his pockets, clenched his teeth and felt his jaw tense. He kept walking, looking around for a shady spot to rest in. He eventually found one behind a large boulder. But the spot was taken! Another man was already lying there. A man with darker skin than his – it was the Arab. Involuntarily, helplessly, he took a step in the other man's direction. The veins were throbbing underneath his skin, beads of sweat were gathering in his eyebrows, the beach was vibrating in the harsh light. He fumbled for the gun in his jacket pocket – and suddenly his entire world is upended:

> The sea carried up a thick, fiery breath. It seemed to me as if the sky split open from one end to the other to rain down fire. My whole being tensed and I squeezed my hand around the revolver. The trigger gave; I felt the smooth underside of the butt; and there, in that noise, sharp and deafening at the same time, is where it all started. I shook off the sweat and sun. I knew that I had shattered the harmony of the day, the exceptional silence of a beach where I'd been happy. Then I fired four more times...

The Mediterranean is perhaps the sea that, more than any other, attracts terror. At least in the world of literature. Take, for instance, Malouf's short story *A Change of Scene*, in which a series of senseless acts of violence spoil an American family's vacation in Greece's mythological, sun-drenched archipelago. Or Thomas Mann's *Mario and the Magician*, in which the magician Cipolla is shot dead – here too, for rather murky reasons – in an Italian seaside town. (It happens after the beautiful summer weather has been pushed aside by a prickly, oppressive scirocco; at the time of the magician's arrival, the sea looks more like a colourless, viscous mass full of stinging jellyfish.) Or, Marguerite Duras' *The Little Horses of Tarquinia*, in which a Mediterranean summer is unsettlingly framed by the death of a young man who's blown up by a landmine the day before the summer guests arrive; the town's nightlife is shut down out of respect for the dead man's parents (who have gathered up the remains of their son's body and placed them in an old soap box but can't bring themselves to leave that place of death).

But what about the Cook Islands? Surely those paradisical beaches do exist? The pictures illustrating the newspaper article are undeniably beautiful. I study them for a long, long time while my mind wanders. I think about Captain Cook, who, having just turned fifty, met his cruel fate in the Pacific. It was in February 1779. The crew was planning their departure from Hawaii. But the morning before they were to cast off, the Europeans made a troubling discovery: one of their small cutters was missing! Cook flew into a rage, assuming the natives had stolen it. He loaded his double-barrel rifle and set off with a handful of crewmembers to find the local chieftain, Kalani'opu'u. They found him on the beach of Kealakekua Bay. The chieftain was keen to avoid conflict with the westerners and promised he would make sure the stolen boat was returned. But while Cook and the chieftain negotiated on the beach, unwelcome news reached them: on the other side of the bay, some of Cook's men had got into an argument with a group of islanders – and had accidentally killed a person of some importance. The Hawaiians were understandably upset – and blamed Cook.

Suddenly, Cook found himself surrounded by hundreds of angry natives. One of them, armed with a large rock and a spear, pushed his way to the captain, who was terrified. He raised his rifle, aimed at the armed man – and fired. He missed, but the tension among the assembled grew. Someone pulled out a knife and attacked one of the British – who parried by striking the man hard in the face with the butt of his rifle. The islanders responded by picking up rocks from the ground and bombarding the strangers.

Cook fired his rifle again, into the crowd.

This time, he didn't miss – and he killed a man. But the situation was already untenable. An enraged islander rushed up to Cook and stabbed him in the shoulder. Another man bludgeoned him from behind. Cook fell flat on his face at the water's edge. "On seeing him fall, the islanders set up a great shout," James King, one of the officers present at the scene, later wrote in his diary. "Snatching the dagger out of each other's hands, they showed a savage eagerness to have a share in his destruction."

Thus, Captain Cook perished on a Hawaiian beach. But the people who would ultimately pay the price of the West's

intrusion into the Pacific were, needless to say, the islanders themselves. Cook's meticulous mapping of the Pacific set the stage for its doom. It started with British penal colonies on the east coast of Australia and Van Diemen's Land (Tasmania). The circumstances involved explain the title of the standard history on the subject, Robert Hughes' *The Fatal Shore*. Inspired by Britain, France established similar prison camps on New Caledonia. Large-scale human trafficking and a merciless exploitation of the islands' natural resources followed. The natives and their environments were broken down bit by bit. In many places in the South Pacific, local populations were reduced by over ninety percent.

That is why the population of Aitutaki is only 2,000 today.

And yet, the western idea of the South Pacific as a paradise on Earth lived on. In fin-de-siècle Europe, it was confirmed by countless travelogues, as well as by a flood of handbills and pamphlets printed by regents, missionaries and businessmen to help recruit volunteers for their colonisation projects. Very few of those volunteers found the paradise they had been promised. Like the native population, the colonisers often saw their new societies collapse as a result of ignorance, failed crops, malaria, conflict with the islanders, internal strife and whatever else. "What a disappointment!" as one frustrated colonist put it. "Our paradise turned into a hell."

In our own century, the beach remains a place with strongly negative connotations for many South Pacific islanders. Beyond the tourist beaches, Le Clézio notes, the coast is often "an area of physical and cultural decay". The mood is "grey and joyless". "What strikes the visitor when he steps onto these beaches is their bleak and hostile appearance". Outside of the tourist resorts, a sense of abandonment and dejection hangs over the borderland that is the beach. The locals choose to make their homes on the heights rather than the beaches.

It's as though they "have made their minds up to forget the sea".

8

The Bluff

There's one Baltic beach that's unlike all the others; it's located on Stora Karlsö, at the foot of a vertical limestone cliff. The beach consists entirely of shingles, rich in fossils. A narrow wooden jetty points the way out into the frigid sea. Sharp-edged rocks litter the water's edge. They were once, one may surmise, part of the cliff; now the gulls perch on them while they gaze out across the Baltic. Higher up the beach, next to the leafy copses huddling at the foot of the cliff wall, is a hunting cabin built in the nineteenth century by a certain

Willy Wöhler, who also founded the company that owns the island these days. Next to the cabin is the equally historic lighthouse keeper's cottage. Both houses are now hostels.

I've visited Stora Karlsö several times over the years, but one stay in particular stands out. It was soon after Midsummer 2010, and M. and I had signed up as volunteers for the annual ring marking of the common murre, the large seabirds that at that time of year breed in large colonies on the island's cliffs. Since a few years before, researchers had, to the great joy of the public, relied on volunteers to undertake that project. It was a rare opportunity to get up close and personal with the birds of Stora Karlsö.

The ring marking took place at dusk, and while waiting for it to begin, we sat on the beach outside the hostel, where we'd made ourselves at home, and watched the darkening sea. The summer night couldn't have been more beautiful, and we took it in with all our senses. The shingles underneath us were warm after a long day of scorching sun. The slackening breeze brought with it a sweet smell of seaweed and brackish water. Before us, Hien Bay spread out like an oily, blueish mirror and behind us, from the sheer cliff face, we heard the pleasant sound of birdsong and chirping insects. The cliff itself, 150 feet tall, gradually turned into a silhouette, its craggy outline sharply drawn against the blush of twilight.

Suddenly, however, the idyll was disturbed by a din that seemed sorely out of place. The noise grew in volume and turned into hollering. Turning my head, I spotted a group of boys who were racing down the stony path from Norderhamn. Presumably, they were part of some youth group camping on the island. Now, they thundered past, bursting with the kind of energy children are often full of just before bedtime. Unparalleled excitement lit up their faces and loud shouts echoed up the cliff wall. The group set their course for a set of stone steps that led up the peak through a patch of very dense trees. A while later, we could see them up at the top. They were dancing and jumping around on the limestone bluff – indeed, dangerously close to the deadly drop. Oh my god! I thought. They're going to fall!

The scene brought to mind *Lord of the Flies*, William Golding's classic in which a group of British boys are forced to fend for themselves on a tropical island. With the athletic Ralph as their natural leader, the boys try to maintain and recreate the civilisation they grew up in. But in stark contrast with R. M. Ballantyne's *The Coral Island* (1858), which Golding was parodying, their primitive instincts soon take over. A break-away faction challenges Ralph's leadership, and the supposedly enlightened and civilised westerners lose themselves in evil and barbarity. The novel's title is a translation of the Hebrew word *Beelzebub*, one of the incarnations of Satan in the New Testament.

The dancing boys at the top of the bluff hardly looked evil, but the sight of them inevitably recalled the dramatic climax of Golding's novel. It revolves around two deaths. The first occurs one night when a thunderstorm sweeps in, bringing torrential rain. The break-away faction, led by a boy called Jack, do a peculiar dance on the tall cliffs that rise up above the sea. One of the boys pretends to be a pig. He gets down on all fours and grunts at the others, who dance around him in a circle, brandishing crude wooden spears and cudgels. The boy in the middle performs the pig's fear of dying. The others shout: "Kill the beast! Cut his throat! Spill his blood!" The boy playing the pig eventually grows tired of his role and joins the others in the circle. But then another, younger boy arrives. He has been in the forest and seems to have something important to say. No one listens. Instead, the human circle closes around the new arrival. The children pick up the chant again: "Kill the beast! Cut his throat! Spill its blood!" And then the unspeakable happens:

> The sticks fell and the mouth of the new circle crunched and screamed. The beast was on his knees in the centre, its arms folded over its face… The beast struggled forward, broke the ring and fell over the steep edge of the rock to the sand by the water. At once the crowd surged after it, poured down the rock, leapt on to the beast, screamed, struck, bit, tore. There were no words, and no movements but the tearing of teeth and claws.

A few days later, the boys return to the top of the cliff. Ralph and Jack fight. Ralph makes one last attempt at persuading the others of the advantages of maintaining law and order, of thinking rationally and keeping the signal fire, which could make a passing ship come to the their rescue, alive. Ralph's speech is met with loud booing. Just then, an ominous rumbling is heard from higher up the slope: an enormous boulder has for some reason broken free and started rolling. It comes straight for Ralph's closest ally, Piggy:

The rock struck Piggy a glancing blow from chin to knee... Piggy, saying nothing, with no time for even a grunt, travelled through the air sideways from the rock, turning over as he went. The rock bounded twice and was lost in the forest. Piggy fell forty feet and landed on his back across that square, red rock in the sea. His head opened and stuff came out and turned red. Piggy's arms and legs twitched a bit, like a pig's after it has been killed. Then the sea breathed again in a long slow sigh, the water boiled white and pink over the rock; and when it went, sucking back again, the body of Piggy was gone.

The boys on the bluff eventually left, and the pleasant calm of the summer night returned. I checked my watch, but it still wasn't time for our ring marking assignment. So we stayed on the beach a while longer.

For centuries, authors like Golding have imagined people who for one reason or another fall off cliffs and are either smashed against rocky shores or swept out to sea. The trend reached its peak during the nineteenth century. On the British Isles, with their many rocky stretches of coast, virtually every single nineteenth and twentieth century author – from Sir Walter Scott and Thomas Hardy to Virginia Woolf and Graham Greene – seems to have explored this brutal form of beach death. And it is, needless to say, ubiquitous in modern crime fiction. When Mari Jungstedt situates some of her characters on Stora Karlsö in *The Double Silence*, it's not long before the limestone bluff's demons rear their ugly heads and a film director is pushed from one of the nesting cliffs – and dies on the shingle beach. "He just fell, his body bounced off several rocky outcrops before it hit the ground. And the birds went flying in every direction." The night before his fall, the victim had participated in the annual ring marking of the common murre.

But as I recalled the gruesome death scenes in Golding's novel, it was impossible not to also remember an oft-cited story from the Bible. It takes place in the land of the Gerasenes, on the shores of the Sea of Galilee. Jesus has just arrived by boat from the other side of the lake, Mark tells us, but he barely has time to disembark before being accosted by "a man with an unclean spirit". The man claims to be named Legion, "for we are many". He pleads with Jesus not to drive his people from the region. He points to a large herd of swine grazing on a nearby mountain. The unclean spirits ask Jesus: "send us into the swine, so that we may enter into them!" And then the miracle happens:

> And the unclean spirits went out, and entered into the
> swine: and the herd ran violently down a steep place into
> the sea, (they were about two thousand;) and were choked in
> the sea.

This wild story, which in time would come to inspire, among others, Fyodor Dostoevsky in *The Possessed*, is often referred to as one of Shakespeare's sources for his play *King Lear*, in which the mountain by the Sea of Galilee has been transformed into the white cliffs of Dover. I've always been fascinated by this drama, in which the king – on account of his advanced

age – cedes his kingdom to two of his three daughters, Goneril and Regan. His daughters' lust for power takes increasingly evil expressions and Lear is driven into a labyrinth of spiralling insanity. The Earl of Gloucester, one of the king's closest allies and confidantes, objects to the King's daughters' disrespectful treatment of their father. Gloucester is himself facing a family crisis that escalates when his bastard son Edmund tries to get rid of the Earl's legitimate heir Edgar. Edmund manages to trick his father into disowning Edgar. Then he sees to it that Gloucester is arrested. Regan and her husband, the Duke of Cornwall, gouge out Gloucester's eyes in a extraordinary act of malice – and then send him out onto a dark highland heath near Dover. There, he meets Edgar, in the disguise of a mad, demon-possessed beggar by the name of Tom. Edgar plays his deranged part with conviction, especially when he accounts for how the evil spirit came to possess him:

> Five fiends have been in poor Tom at once; of lust, as Obidicut;
> Hobbididence, prince of dumbness; Mahu, of stealing; Modo,
> of murder; Flibbertigibbet, of mopping and mowing.

After all the evil that has befallen him, Gloucester decides to take his own life. When he meets his son, he asks him for help, not recognising who he really is:

> Dost thou know Dover?
> There is a cliff, whose high and bending head
> Looks fearfully in the confined deep:
> Bring me but to the very brim of it,
> And I'll repair the misery thou dost bear
> With something rich about me: from that place
> I shall no leading need.

Then he takes the beggar's hand and lets himself be led toward the sheer drop – or so he believes. After walking for some time, the demon-possessed beggar stops and says to the blind man:

> Come on, sir; here's the place: stand still. How fearful
> And dizzy 'tis, to cast one's eyes so low!
> The crows and choughs that wing the midway air
> Show scarce so gross as beetles: half way down
> Hangs one that gathers samphire, dreadful trade!
> Methinks he seems no bigger than his head:
> The fishermen, that walk upon the beach,
> Appear like mice; and yond tall anchoring bark,
> Diminish'd to her cock; her cock, a buoy
> Almost too small for sight: the murmuring surge,
> That on the unnumber'd idle pebbles chafes,
> Cannot be heard so high. I'll look no more;
> Lest my brain turn, and the deficient sight
> Topple down headlong.

And with that, Gloucester believes he has reached the end of the road. He asks the beggar to take him right up to the precipice. Shakespeare then writes in his stage directions that Gloucester leaps straight out – and falls headlong on the ground! Because Tom the Fool hasn't taken him to the edge of the abyss; they're both still safe on the heath. But with that "fall", Tom is transformed, as though the demons have been exorcised. It is now Edgar, not Tom, who speaks. He explains to Gloucester that he has jumped off the cliff and landed on the

When murre hatchlings reach the age of three weeks, they jump from their nests on the cliffs of Stora Karlsö – a fall of over one hundred feet. They don't want to do it, but they have no other choice. Their mothers and fathers try to convince them they can fly. They can't, of course, because their wings haven't developed yet. The mothers fly in circles just off the cliff, encouraging their young to take the plunge. The fathers bob on the waves shouting it's time. The chicks still don't want to. But in the end, they do it anyway. Always at dusk, when the hungry gulls, with their poor eyesight, can't get them.

It was time for us to get to work. We climbed down a rickety ladder from the bluff to the shingle beach on the north side of the island. The summer night was settling over the sea. The Baltic roared in the stiff breeze, which was considerably more intense on this side, but it found competition in the deafening screeching of thousands upon thousands of birds. We were ready. A brief dull thud marked the moment the first murre chick landed next to me. It lay there for a moment, battered and in shock. But it wasn't dead. Before long, it came to. Still dizzy from the violent fall, it took a few staggering steps. It moved in a daze. Off it went along a meandering path, between rocks, through narrow gaps. Quickly, furiously, it tottered on with its webbed little legs, crying in a shrill, squeaky voice. Its young body, so it appeared to me, was brimming with energy. It twisted and turned when I picked it up, looked at me with frustrated, childish eyes. I wrapped my hands around the bird's wings and yielding ribcage, around the soft, downy feathers. It could live for twenty years, maybe longer if it stayed safe – and in time, it might return here, to Stora Karlsö, to raise its own family. But right now, it just wanted to get away, away from the prison of my hands.

Away from the rocky beach, to the freedom of the sea.

9

In the Tidal Zone

One of the better but somewhat overlooked films at the Stockholm Film Festival in 2009 was a Latin American production with the evocative title *Marea de arena*. The director was Mexican, Gustavo Montiel Pagés, but the story took place on the Atlantic shores of Argentina and in the barren deserts of Patagonia. In this periphery, we find emotional photographer Juan and his beautiful wife Mar. Sadly, their marriage is unhappy and they have recently separated. Now, they each live in a small house by the sea, their only remaining link their son Martin.

The boy likes the sea, the big blue that shares a name with his mother. Juan is more ambivalent. The waves, the whales, the octopuses – they all seem to be in cahoots with his rival: marine biologist Sebastian, Mar's new boyfriend. When he looks out at the gloomy, grey water, he laments that his love for Mar is no longer requited, that he can't get through to the person he loves. Jealousy takes root inside him. He seeks solace in the dunes, where the wind stirs up the sand in great swirls. Juan's new book, in which his ex-wife poses against a backdrop of sand, is ambiguously entitled *Mar de arena*.

But *marea*, as in the film's title, is quite different from *mar*: it means tide.

Ocean tides are caused by the gravitational pull of the moon and the sun, but the rationality of this explanation hasn't stopped humanity from fearing the ebb and flow of the sea; the laws of gravity haven't been much help for people who find themselves on the wrong beach at the wrong time. Coastal cliffs of various kinds have appeared particularly terrifying in this respect. I remember, for example, a trip to the beautiful island of Rügen, off the Baltic coast of Germany. I'd come there in the company of my English friend Gary, whose great passion in life is rambling. We'd planned to hike along the seashore from the train station in Sassnitz up toward Cape Arkona, the ancient haunt of the Danes in the south Baltic. This was not just any hike, because next to the narrow stone beach loomed the famed chalk cliffs of Rügen. The white cliffs were truly imposing; in places, they rise to 230 feet. Climbing

them without equipment would have been as impossible as scaling the nesting cliffs of Stora Karlsö.

We were about halfway to Cape Arkona when Gary to my surprise exclaimed: "We can't forget about the tides!" At first, I didn't understand what he meant. Back then, my own beach adventures were confined to the shallow inland sea of the Baltic, which certainly holds some dangers of its own, but which in terms of tides is for all intents and purposes cut off from the ebbs and flows of the ocean. Nevertheless, Gary's face expressed genuine worry. I tried to reassure him by telling him what I knew; that the Danish sounds were far too narrow to allow tides to surge through, that the water level of the Baltic was more or less constant and that we therefore had nothing to fear. But even though Gary accepted this explanation on a logical level, the concerned look in his eyes remained.

For the British, islanders as they are, a fear of the tide may be genetic. Many Britons have stories about some forebear who in the distant past fell prey to its whims. Death by tide is a variation on the death-by-drowning theme, but the roles are reversed: here, it's not that the beachgoer wades out into the sea, swims away and disappears. Here, the ocean swells and swallows up people who ought to be safe on the beach; unless they've been trapped and drowned in some too-low-lying cave, as in the Tintin adventure *The Black Island*. The British have always been keenly aware of this danger, particularly since the middle of the eighteenth century, when going to the beach became fashionable. Witnessing the rising of the tide with one's own eyes, as every seaside visitor did, was a powerful experience for a lot of Britons, not least because they inevitably made a mental connection between the swell of the ocean and the Biblical story of the Flood.

Hardly surprisingly, such experiences left their mark in literature. The first author to deal seriously with the tidal theme was probably George Crabbe, whose *The Borough* (1810) – later reworked by Benjamin Britten into the opera *Peter Grimes* (1945) – portrays life in a small English coastal town. The most popular pastime in the town, which shares many characteristics with Crabbe's (and Britten's) hometown Aldeburgh in Suffolk, is promenading along the beach while admiring the sea, this natural wonder that humans also have good reason to fear:

> Then may the poorest with the wealthy look
> On ocean, glorious page of Nature's book!
> May see its varying views in every hour,
> All softness now, then rising with new power,
> As sleeping to invite, or threat'ning to devour:
> 'Tis this which gives us all our choicest views;
> Its waters heal us, and its shores amuse.
>
> See! those fair nymphs upon that rising strand,
> Yon long salt lake has parted from the strand;
> Well pleased to press that path, so clean, so pure,
> To seem in danger, yet to feel secure;
> Trifling with terror, while they strive to shun
> The curling billows; laughing as they run;
> They know the neck that joins the shore and sea,
> Or, ah! how changed that fearless laugh would be.

On Sundays – if the sea is calm – the residents of the town sometimes charter rowboats to take them out to a small nearby island, which is in reality little more than a shoal revealed only at low tide. It is, in other words, important to be mindful of ebb and flow. One Sunday, things almost end in disaster. A group arrives on the island, disembark and pull their boat up on the shore. Spirits are high, a cooling breeze is blowing; it's a lovely summer day by the sea. They play games, dance and sing, have tea and collect seashells. But then someone discovers, to everyone's dismay, that the rowboat they came in is gone! As it turns out, the boatman and his mate have drunk themselves into a stupor and allowed the boat to drift away.

Everyone knows what this loss means. They rebuke the boatman and his mate, but that changes nothing, of course. Instead, they decide to shout for help, in the hope that someone on the nearby – yet so hopelessly remote – mainland might hear. They call out once, twice, three times, all together, as loudly as they can, and eagerly listen for a response. But no one answers their calls, the only sounds are the wind, the lapping of the waves, the dissonant screeching of the gulls. And then the inevitable happens: the tide starts rolling in.

> Foot after foot on the contracted ground
> The billows fall, and dreadful is the sound;
> Less and yet less the sinking isle became,
> And there was wailing, weeping, wrath and blame.

The water level rises, though from the perspective of the people trapped on the sandy island, it seems rather like it's sinking into the sea. The sun sets, night falls. The sea is wet and cold. In the end, the entire island has been engulfed by the waves. The water is now waist-high on the adults. The children are crying. The water continues to rise. Death creeps closer.

Someone suggests they jointly cry out for help, one last time. Their shout rings out through the purple dusk. And – miracle of miracles, a sound is heard: an oar! Some sailors have spotted the abandoned boat, drifting on the waves and come to the rescue. Death leaves empty-handed this time – but each and every one now knows what it feels like to, as another poet would later put it, have low beaches.

George Crabbe had many readers in his day, one of whom was Sir Walter Scott. Scott was fascinated with the description of the tide in *The Borough* and by relocating it to the coast of Scotland, which is considerably craggier than that of Suffolk, he established the archetypal tidal drama in British literature. It's contained in Scott's novel *The Antiquary* (1816), which opens with the arrival of an enigmatic young nobleman by the name of Lovel. On his journey to the Scottish coast, he has struck up an acquaintance with antiquary Jonathan Oldbuck. Oldbuck likes Lovel and decides to introduce him to his friend Sir Arthur Wardour. When Sir Arthur arrives at Oldbuck's home, he brings with him his beautiful daughter Isabella, who to her surprise realises she already knows Lovel. They were once secretly in love – but that was a long time ago and she is not happy to see him. In order to avoid his company on the way home, Isabella therefore persuades her father to take a longer route back to their house, along the shore.

It's a lovely summer night. Father and daughter stroll quietly side by side along the deserted beach, rounding a point and then another, and another. At first, they feel they have nothing to fear. But there's a change in weather in the offing: the restless flight of the jackdaws signals an approaching storm. And then the tide starts to come in, slowly but inexorably, in gleaming silver billows. Isabella now regrets coming down to the shore. Her father tries to soothe her, but his hurried steps is proof he's far from unperturbed himself. Then, they see a figure running toward them. The figure is gesticulating wildly. It's a beggar they know, Edie Ochiltree. He has come to warn them. "Turn back! Turn back!" he calls. He points at the incoming tide; it's already high enough to block their path around the next point! But when they turn around, they discover that the path behind them has been cut off, too. And the water continues to rise:

> The howling of the storm mingled with the shrieks of the seafowl, and sounded like the dirge of the three devoted beings, who, pent between two of the most magnificent, yet most dreadful objects of nature – a raging tide and an insurmountable precipice – toiled along their painful and dangerous path, often lashed by the spray of some giant billow, which threw itself higher on the beach than those that had preceded it. Each minute did their enemy gain ground perceptibly upon them!

Edie Ochiltree points to a cliff they might be able to climb. It looks like it should be out of the tide's reach. But when they reach the cliff, it, too has disappeared beneath the surface! The three are filled with dread and deepest despair. "My child! My child! – to die such a death!" Sir Arthur exclaims. They stop, exhausted at the highest point they can find.

> Here, then, they were to await the sure though slow progress of the raging element, something in the situation of the martyrs of the early church, who, exposed by heathen tyrants to be slain by wild beasts, were compelled for a time to witness the impatience and rage by which the animals were agitated, while awaiting the signal for undoing their grates, and letting them loose upon the victims.

But is there truly no escape? young Isabella cries. Is there no way to scale the steep cliff? No, it really does seem impossible. But then, just as all hope seems lost, their saviour appears on the cliff above them – it's Lovel! And he has brought a sturdy rope. Soon, the three of them are safe. At the last second, too: as they look back down at the outcrop where they were standing mere seconds earlier, the tide has already engulfed it. The drama of that night marks the beginning of a new, trusting relationship between Sir Arthur, Isabella and Lovel.

While British tidal scenes from that era were often set on the craggy coast of Scotland, where people's primary fear was to be cornered and trapped when the tide came in, on the other side of the English Channel, in France, they dreaded quicksand more. Quicksand was common on the British Isles as well, where it found its way into stories like Robert Louis Stevenson's *The Pavilion on the Links* and Sir Arthur Conan Doyle's *The Hound of the Baskervilles*. But in France, the quicksand theme resonated more profoundly and became a metaphor for contemporary political and social turbulence. The privileged classes in particular were – post 1789 – painfully aware that there was, figuratively speaking, no firm ground underneath their feet. It could give way at any moment, and no one was safe; the traumatic events of the French Revolution and the Reign of Terror had proven as much.

Along the French Atlantic coast, on the other hand, especially along the shores of the Bay of Biscay, quicksand was a very real danger. As sea bathing became fashionable in France, the number of incidents rose steadily year on year. A general fear of sand spread through French society and almost every day the newspapers printed articles about tragic deaths in the treacherous borderland between land and sea. The following tragedy, which author François-Marie-Guillaume Habasque claimed to have witnessed one night in 1828 on the coast between Ploulec'h and Lannion in Brittany, is a typical example from this time:

> People were dancing in a circle on this treacherous shore (between Ploulech and Lannion). Suddenly, the mobile ground on which they stood disappeared from beneath the feet of a young maiden. A captain of the merchant marine to whom she was engaged rushed over and saved her, but he himself died, a victim of his devotion. A young man aspiring to become a notary also perished on this occasion.

The event is by all accounts made up, because being swallowed whole by quicksand is impossible, contrary to the claims of many stories (the most well-known of which may be the quicksand scene in Victor Hugo's *Les Misérables*). All the more real was the risk of getting *stuck* in quicksand, which could have dire consequences for the beachgoer who was unable to call for help in time – which is to say before the tide came in. In the early nineteenth century, a number of stories about such tragedies made the rounds in French society, many of which took place on the beaches around the island of Noirmoutier near Nantes. At low tide, it was possible to walk out to this island without one's shoes getting wet, but it was considered prudent to engage a local guide with practical knowledge of the dangers of the bay.

In one case, a group of townsfolk had spent the day on Noirmoutier. As evening began to fall, they prepared to return to the mainland. They hired a sand guide who led them through the tidal zone. But halfway across, the guide grew concerned. He lay down, pressed his ear against the sand and listened. When he stood back up, his face shone with terror. "The tide, my boys!" he shouted. "The tide is coming in! Run! Do you hear me? Run!" Rouget de Kerguen, who recounted this purportedly self-experienced event, goes on:

> The sand was already moving, the mud was already shaking under our heavy steps. A profound terror grabbed hold of us. We heard the sea roaring in the background: it was perhaps a league away, and we perhaps half an hour from death … I could see the Ocean opening its gaping jaw to devour us.

The mainland is still far away, too far. In the end, the distraught men are forced to climb onto a buoy in the bay. To that, they then manage to cling until the next morning, when a fishing boat picks them up. But one of the men is missing. He fell behind during the mad dash, got stuck in quicksand and was drowned by the tide.

The fear of getting stuck in quicksand and drowning in the incoming tide was so widespread in France many resort guests from the upper classes panicked at the slightest sign of instability. While the danger was often imagined, the panic it caused occasionally had tragic consequences. In 1820, for instance, there's a report of a tragedy that began with three ladies who had been sea bathing. Suddenly, they felt, or imagined feeling, that the sandy bottom no longer supported them – and in the chaos that ensued they all drowned – though it was afterwards confirmed that the seabed showed no trace of quicksand. A similar case was reported in 1833 when two bathing women were seized by the same hysterical fear of the sand, at which point one of them fell over in the water and could only just be saved.

The tide has continued to claim victims even in our own time. Just last week, I read in a British newspaper about a tragedy that rivals *The Borough* and the quicksand tragedies of nineteenth century France. It was the hottest day of the year in England. People were flocking to the seaside. On a beach in Camber Sands, near Brighton, thousands of people were jostling for space, among them five young, happy men who had recently immigrated from Sri Lanka. They'd brought a football and went out to a large, flat sand island that had appeared a few hundred yards from the beach proper. It would be hard to imagine a better spot for a game of beach footie. They played, laughed and enjoyed each other's company. And time passed. Then they noticed the tide was coming in. They hurried back toward the shore. On their way, the seabed gave way under two of the men. They sank into sand and got stuck. Their friends rushed back to save them, but that turned out to be very difficult indeed. Both men were too firmly trapped. The tide was coming in fast. Then a strong undertow swept away the three men who were trying to free their friends. None of them knew how to swim – and so, they drowned. Rescue services searched frantically for the two men who got stuck, but they weren't found until the tide went back out. Their bodies were still trapped in the quicksand.

In *Marea de arena*, Juan has an eccentric habit: he asks people to bury him in the sand – standing up, all the way to his chin. It's an effective way of soothing and cleansing his body, he explains. But not only that:

> It's a way of anticipating death. To want to see what it feels like. You know, don't you, that the human body has an awful lot of liquids, isn't that so? In fact, when you stay still all movement in the container that is the body with these liquids also stops and, after a while, a kind of inertia sets in. And when you can't move, the waters we have inside are still, and then you start to become a part of the landscape.

In the final scene, Juan lets Mar bury him in the sand. Ever since Sebastian was found murdered, Juan has been trying to get her back. He believes Mar doesn't know the truth: that it was her ex-husband who, in a fit of jealousy, shot and killed Sebastian. But she does know. And it's time for revenge.

Juan's head is sticking out of the grey sand. Dark cloud shadows race across the beach. Mar puts the shovel down and studies the buried man one last time. Then she walks away. She picks up Martin, climbs into her ex-husband's jeep and drives away. Juan is alone on the beach, buried up to his neck. Eventually, the tide comes creeping in. The sun is setting, the cliffs cast long shadows. Now, the first wave reaches him. The water rises slowly. He can still gasp for breath between the waves. But not for long.

In the end, Juan is gone, swallowed by the sea.

10

A Realm of Sorrow

October in the Netherlands. The bathing season is long since over, but in the evening, there are still a lot of people on the beaches of the North Sea: people who, seemingly under the influence of some mystical force, have felt compelled to seek out the sea as the day draws to a close. I watch them as they stroll along the water's edge. Sometimes, they stop for a moment to dream themselves away, out across the water, toward the clouds and the greyish-blue horizon. They stand there looking contemplative, like the characters in the Caspar David Friedrich painting: pondering their own existence, life as they have lived it. At least that's what I imagine. It's hardly a coincidence, I muse, that we often picture the past as a dark body of water, an ocean of events, densely packed droplets of everything we were once but never can be again. In our memories, we can dive into it, dig around the rocks at the bottom and, at our own risk, bring this one or that back up to the present. "I feel something start within me," Proust writes, "something that leaves its resting-place and attempts to rise, something that has been embedded like an anchor at a great depth; I do not know yet what it is, but I can feel it mounting slowly; I can measure the resistance, I can hear the echo of great spaces traversed."

In *The Beach*, Richard believes the beach has an "amnesiac effect" – that it induces memory loss. After just a few days in the secluded paradise, with its palm trees, coral reefs and turquoise water, he senses that his memory "begins to shut itself down". Memories of his past become blurred. Before long, it's as though it never existed, the life he once lived; it's as though he has always lived here, on the beach.

Many of us have experienced that amnesiac effect, the exhilarating feeling of having escaped our past, escaped history, on the beach. Isn't that the underlying purpose of our seaside vacations: to forget our sorrows, escape the niggling problems of everyday life? And isn't a sandy beach physically designed to achieve this? I take off my socks and shoes, roll up my trousers and walk down to the water's edge. I let the waves wash over my feet – and watch as they quickly erase my footprints. I think about the beach artist I saw here this morning, a tanned man of about forty-five who, not unlike Peter Kihlgård's beach man, had made the beach his studio. All day long, he threw himself into his sand art, "painting" the sand, creating intricate sand sculptures. I can still make out some of them in the twilight. But tomorrow, his sculptures will have been destroyed and his beautiful "paintings" washed away by the tide. There will be no trace of yesterday, and that's a good thing, because it means art can spring forth anew, without reference to what came before. The beach is freedom. The beach is forgetting.

Paradoxically, the seashore also functions as a domain of remembrance, a zone that awakens the past in the form of painful memories. It's during a visit to Balbec, a fictional seaside town on the coast of Normandy, that Proust's narrator suddenly "discovers" that his beloved grandmother is no longer among the living – even though she has already been dead for over a year at that point! Significantly, the realisation comes as he notices the sea view from his hotel room. He remembers his grandmother's reassuring presence during previous summers in Balbec. Now, when he wants to embrace her and shower her with kisses once more, he realises it's impossible – "I had only just discovered this because I had only just, on feeling her for the first time, alive, authentic, making my heart swell to breaking-point, on finding her at last, learned that I had lost her for ever."

He struggles with the painful "contradiction of memory and nonexistence", which is to say between remembering a loved one and knowing that she is no longer there, that she never will be there again. At the hotel, he habitually closes his shutters, because he can't "bear to have before my eyes those waves of the sea which my grandmother could formerly contemplate for hours on end; the fresh image of their heedless

My grandmother appeared to me, seated in an armchair. So feeble she was, she seemed to be less alive than other people. And yet I could hear her breathe; now and again she made a sign to show that she had understood what we were saying, my father and I. But in vain might I take her in my arms, I failed utterly to kindle a spark of affection in her eyes, a flush of colour in her cheeks. Absent from herself, she appeared somehow not to love me, not to know me, perhaps not to see me. I could not interpret the secret of her indifference, of her dejection, of her silent resentment. I drew my father aside. "You can see, all the same," I said to him, "there's no doubt about it, she understands everything perfectly. It is a perfect imitation of life. If we could have your cousin here, who maintains that the dead don't live. Why, she's been dead for more than a year now, and she's still alive. But why won't she give me a kiss?" – "Look her poor head is drooping again." – "But she wants to go, now, to the Champs-Elysées." – "It's madness!" – "You really think it can do her any harm, that she can die any further? It isn't possible that she no longer loves me. I keep on hugging her, won't she ever smile at me again?" – "What can you expect, when people are dead they are dead."

Half a century older is Hans Christian Andersen's sad story about *Anne Lisbeth*, who at a young age gives birth to an ugly, illegitimate child whom she gives away to a ditch digger's wife and then pushes from her mind. Many years later, however, as she passes through the region where she grew up, she takes the opportunity to visit with her child's foster parents. They tell her the boy, who went to sea a few years earlier, recently perished in a shipwreck. Anne Lisbeth shrugs and nothing more is said. But that night, she decides to walk back home along the beach – much like the Wardours in *The Antiquary* – and she is deep in thought. The secretive borderland between land and sea does something to her, compels her to reflect and see her life as though from the outside – and remember. She walks in a daze, but her mind is racing: thoughts about God, about sin, about conscience, about life and death. Her mind becomes "clear for thoughts that had never before been there".

The summer night darkens, but the beach is illuminated by the moon. Suddenly, she pulls up short, frightened by something strange at the water's edge: grass and tangled seaweed have wrapped themselves around an oblong stone; it looks "just like a corpse". She walks on, but before long she recalls the stories from her childhood, the superstition about the "spectres of the seashore", the ghosts of drowned, unburied sailors washed up on desolate beaches. Their bodies, she knows, are harmless, but their spirits pursue lonely wanderers, clinging to them, demanding to be carried to the churchyard to be buried in consecrated soil. Anne Lisbeth thinks about her child, "her own child, whom she had never loved, nor ever given any thought", and pictures this child dead at the bottom of the sea. She imagines what it would be like if his spectre appeared.

As these thoughts passed through her mind, fear gave speed to her feet, so that she walked faster and faster. Fear came upon her as if a cold, clammy hand had been laid upon her heart, so that she almost fainted. As she looked across the sea, all there grew darker; a heavy mist came rolling onwards, and clung to bush and tree, distorting them into fantastic shapes. She turned and glanced at the moon, which had risen behind her. It looked like a pale, rayless surface, and a deadly weight seemed to hang upon her limbs. "Hold," thought she; and then she turned round a second time to look at the moon. A white face appeared quite close to her, with a mist, hanging like a garment from its shoulders. "Stop! carry me to consecrated earth," sounded in her ears, in strange, hollow tones. The sound did not come from frogs or ravens; she saw no sign of such creatures. "A grave! dig me a grave!" was repeated quite loud. Yes, it was indeed the spectre of her child. The child that lay beneath the ocean, and whose spirit could have no rest until it was carried to the churchyard, and until a grave had been dug for it in consecrated ground.

Anne Lisbeth decides to walk in the direction of the church-yard to dig a grave for her son. The fog is cold and damp, Anne Lisbeth's hands and face cold and damp with fear. Is that the churchyard she sees? Perhaps she's slightly mistaken about the black crosses and black ravens.

And she threw herself upon the earth, and with her hands dug a grave in the hard ground, so that the blood ran from her fingers. "A grave! dig me a grave!" still sounded in her ears; she was fearful that the cock might crow, and the first red streak appear in the east, before she had finished her work; and then she would be lost. And the cock crowed, and the day dawned in the east, and the grave was only half dug. An icy hand passed over her head and face, and down towards her heart. "Only half a grave," a voice wailed, and fled away. Yes, it fled away over the sea; it was the ocean spectre.

Overcome and devastated, Anne Lisbeth collapses senseless on the ground. Late the next morning, she is woken up by two men. But she's not in the churchyard, she's still on the shore, where she has dug a deep hole in the sand in front of her. The men take her back home, but she's a changed person. She's sick, her thoughts "like a confused, tangled skein; only one thread, only one thought was clear to her, namely that she must carry the spectre of the sea-shore to the churchyard, and dig a grave for him there; that by so doing she might win back her soul. Many a night she was missed from her home, and was always found on the sea-shore waiting for the spectre."

It apparently doesn't matter which beach we're on; proximity to the sea seems to evoke painful memories of the dead in every part of the world. The theme is ubiquitous in modern literature, too, from bestsellers like David Baldacci's *One Summer* to Booker Prize winners like John Banville's *The Sea*. One of my favourites in the genre is William Boyd's *Brazzaville Beach*. The heroine of this novel, Hope Clearwater, has after a tumultuous period settled down in a small beach cottage in a fictional country on the Atlantic coast of Africa. She tries to explain to the reader – and herself – how she ended up there:

> I love the beach, but sometimes, I ask myself, what am I doing here? I'm young, I'm single, I have family in England, I possess

all manner of impressive academic qualifications. So why has the beach become my home...? How can I explain it to you? I am here because two sets of strange and extraordinary events happened to me, and I needed some time to weigh them up, evaluate them. I have to make sense of what has taken place, before I can restart my life in the world, as it were. Do you know that feeling? That urge to call a temporary halt, to say: enough, slow down, give me a break.

One of the two sets of events is about how she came to Africa to take part in a prestigious research project about the sexual habits of chimpanzees – and about how she was subsequently kidnapped by a group of guerrillas, in whose company she has experienced the heinous realities of civil war up close. But as she sits on the veranda of her beach cottage, these events merge with other recollections. Because she had another reason to come here: she wanted to escape her past. More specifically, she's on the run from the painful memory of her ex-husband, an eccentric mathematician who after the couple's traumatic divorce developed a nervous disorder and took his own life. She thirsts for the amnesiac effect of the beach. But forgetfulness proves elusive.

Banville's *The Sea*, a more poetic work, is about an art historian, Max Morden, whose wife has recently died of cancer. As a means of dealing with his grief, Morden relocates to a remote seaside town he used to visit as a child. He goes there in the hope of recalibrating his devastated existence. But the memories of his distant past make this easier said than done. As he wanders along the familiar roads and footpaths, he recalls the summers of his childhood. He also remembers his childhood friends, Chloe and Myles. It has been decades since he last thought about them, but now the memories resurface: how they played on the beach, his affection for Chloe, the nanny set to watch over them – and how he was separated from his friends under the most tragic of circumstances, as both Chloe and Myles drowned.

In other words, instead of working through the grief of his wife's passing, Morden's haunted by further memories of death. Lost and confused, with a bottle of cognac in his hand, he wanders along the beach that was the scene of the tragedy. He sits down in the cold sand, stretches out his legs and contemplates life, the cruelty of death. He thinks about his dead wife, about his dead childhood friends, and he drinks. The bottle grows lighter, his head heavier. Darkness falls. When the lanterns on a distant ship are lit, he makes a half-hearted attempt to stand up. The lights draw him in. He takes a few staggering steps into the water, wants to wade out and become one with the sea – but trips, falls and hits his head on a rock. There he lies, dipping in and out of consciousness, unable – or unwilling – to move.

> I was not in pain, not even very much upset. In fact, it seemed quite natural to be sprawled there, in the dark, under a tumultuous sky, watching the faint phosphorescence of the waves as they pattered forward eagerly only to retreat again, like a flock of inquisitive mice... and hearing the wind above me blowing through the great invisible hollows and funnels of the air.

The most spectacular of all meetings with the beaches of the past takes place in the science-fiction film *Contact*, based on a novel by Carl Sagan. Astronomer Eleanor Arroway's childhood trauma is the early loss of a beloved father with a weak heart. He passes away one evening just after Ellie, who is a radio enthusiast, manages to make contact with Pensacola in Florida. Many years later, now a professional radio astronomer, she makes contact of a radically different kind: with an alien civilisation. A radio message from space turns out to contain plans for building a spaceship. The vessel is constructed according to the extra-terrestrial instructions and Ellie sets off on an intergalactic journey. She travels through space and time, squeezing through a series of wormholes. She reaches another solar system. The vessel heads for one of the planets and goes in for landing. The planet is unspeakably beautiful; Ellie descends toward a blindingly white beach. The water is light turquoise, the palm trees sway in the tropical breeze. It looks like Earth! she marvels. The only unfamiliar thing is the sky: it's not blue, like back home, but black and strewn with stars. Red and blue nebulas and golden galaxies dance above Ellie's head.

After landing on the beach, she sees a peculiar figure take shape in the distance. At first, the figure is little more than a warping of space, like warm air surrounded by colder. The creature moves toward her. She squints to try to make out what kind of creature it is. Her heart is racing. Then, to her astonishment, she realises it's not an alien. It's a human, and not just any human: it's her late father! He looks exactly like he used to, which is to say: exactly how she remembers him.

I I

Flight

There was an advertisement campaign some years ago that touted Gotland's "fifth season": those pleasant weeks at the end of August and start of September. Big posters in Stockholm's metro extolled its virtues and the internet was flooded with commercials. It was a silly concept, perhaps, like most advertisement concepts – and yet there really was something about that "extra" season on Gotland, when it was neither quite late summer nor early autumn. M. and I lingered in Kvarnåkershamn, which had already emptied of summer visitors. The colours of the landscape had faded a little, the birdsong had fallen silent. But the air was still warm and mild, the sunshine gentle. It was a beautiful and quiet period on the island.

A few days a week, I would drive up to Visby, where I sat in the Almedal Library, reading and writing. I was working on an essay about seafaring in the Baltic around the end of the Second World War. My favourite book on the subject was *Sea of Death* by marine historian Claes-Göran Wetterholm. It was an apt title, because from the autumn of 1944 on, the shores of the Baltic were littered with corpses: men, women and children who, fleeing the cruel reality of the war, had sought to escape by sea – but had never reached the opposite shore. Some had died before they could even leave the coast they were fleeing; the Nazi searchlights that swept the occupied beaches were not only there to catch intruders, but also to spot refugees trying to get away. Those who were seen were shot. We can read about it in academic papers, but also in literary works like Alfred Andersch's *Flight to Afar* or Siegfried Lenz' ironic *Moods of the Sea*. Others perished in the crossing when their boats were sunk by storms or submarines. The legendary sinking of the ship Wilhelm Gustloff – described by authors like Günter Grass in *Crabwalk* and Tanja Dückers in *Celestial bodies* – remains the greatest refugee catastrophe in history. 9,352 people died. Six times more than when the Titanic sank in 1912.

And yet, it wasn't the mass tragedies that touched me the most, it was the little ones, the ones about individual fates. There was hardly a beach around the Baltic that didn't see the corpse of a refugee or soldier wash ashore in the last phase of the war. Even in our own Kvarnåkershamn, as I discovered in an old issue of the local paper, a dead body had been found. The corpse was wearing a German uniform:

It was a man of about 20–25, wearing a life preserver and uniform jacket and full-length leather trousers. The body had by all appearances not been long in the water. No papers or identity markers were found on the dead man, not even a dog tag, but judging by the insignia on the uniform, he seems to have held the rank of sergeant in the navy.

Who was he? Where had he come from? What had he lived through? How had he ended up here? At the funeral service in Silte Church, government officials, military officers and diplomats, Swedish and German, were present. But no one could answer the locals' many questions. They shrugged their shoulders, shook their heads. In the end, one of the villagers, Mrs Helny Koch, rose to speak. She cleared her throat, ran her eyes over the congregants and then read a few verses she had composed herself, which were printed in the paper the next day:

> In this small cemetery
> We have gathered to bury
> A stranger with no name
> Who to our island came
> And returns nevermore
> To his homeland's shore
>
> Where have you been?
> What have you seen?
> The sea brought you here
> The shore was your bier
> The world around you ablaze
> With war and suffering in these darkest of days.

The most heart-breaking tales were the ones about children – fleeing, terrified children who failed to reach safety on the other side of the sea. Like the little Latvian girl, just four years old, who left Courland with her mother and sister on

2 October 1944. That evening, they walked down to the white beach at Kolka. The wind was high. Hand in hand, they climbed into the small fishing boat that had lain hidden among the pine trees for weeks. About fifteen other refugees were already waiting in the boat, mainly women and children. Like most of their Baltic compatriots, they set their course for the east coast of Gotland. But after thirty hours at sea, the boat drifted into Gotska Sandön instead. Night had fallen, a pitch-black autumn night. When the refugees approached the beach at around half past three in the morning, their boat was suddenly upended by a breaker and everyone on board fell into the water. The next wave heaved them ashore. The grownups escaped with minor cuts and bruises. But the four-year-old girl and her seven-year-old sister were found lifeless at the water's edge. The locals had seen the boat from the lighthouse and came running to help. The two children were rushed to the lighthouse keeper's cottage, where the older girl was successfully resuscitated. But the younger child could not be brought back, though they worked on her for three hours. She'd worn a scarf wrapped twice around her neck, tied with double knots. To keep her warm, her distraught mother explained. When she fell into the sea, moisture tightened the knots and the girl suffocated.

In the evenings, on my way back to Kvarnåkershamn, I listened to the radio news, whose reports from the world beyond Gotland often seemed like eerie mirror images of my research at the library. The Second World War may have been over, but in the Middle East, in Afghanistan and in several African countries, other wars still raged, and they were no less cruel. From these living hells – which seemed so remote to me despite news of them reaching me daily – large numbers of people were fleeing. Via Turkey and North Africa, they were trying to reach Europe. But to get there, they had to cross the Mediterranean. They used their life savings to buy their way onto the vessels of people smugglers. Thousands never reached their destination – and like the shores of the Baltic in the 1940s, the beaches of the Mediterranean were now littered with washed-up bodies.

Sometimes, as I drove along the coast of Gotland, I would be overcome with a bizarre conviction that they were all the same people; souls reborn only to have to flee new conflicts, once more desperately trying to cross the sea. Whenever I saw pictures of the overcrowded refugee ships, it was as though I half-expected to spot the young German sergeant, still in his Nazi uniform, holding hands with the little girl from Latvia, her scarf still wrapped too tightly around her neck, fleeing from Turkey or Libya toward a safe haven in the north or west. Because somewhere, I could feel it, they lived on, those men, women and children for whom time had stopped.

One evening, I left Visby later than usual and as a result missed my regular news broadcast. When I turned on the radio, I was instead greeted by a pleasantly deep male voice reading Kristoffer Leandoer's short story *Beach Riders*. I suppose the producer picked it because it tied in with the refugee crisis, which at the time utterly dominated public debate in Sweden. In the story, a young man from Stockholm, Fredrik, travels to Orust to visit his girlfriend, the evasive Albertina. He's fascinated by the sinister stories he's told about the island's past and its intimate relationship with the sea. It turns out Albertina's house is built entirely from the wood of a refugee ship that ran aground on Orust on a dark November night in 1943. Fredrik also learns the shipwreck was no accident; the islanders used false light signals to deliberately lure the ship toward the coast. Then they "defiled" it. The incident is still talked about on Orust.

That night, Fredrik has a terrible nightmare:

> Albertina was coming toward him with her arms outstretched, walking along the water's edge; waves from a raging sea washed over her feet and each one washed up new little bodies; the beach was littered with the corpses of refugee children and Albertina didn't see them, didn't bother lifting her feet to avoid stepping on them.

The next day, Fredrik ventures into Albertina's house. To his surprise, it's "illuminated as if for a party". The rooms are filled with "waiting figures, identical, dripping wet in drab, faded rags, with lifeless grey faces and empty eye sockets that were all turned to him". He smells saltwater and bloated bodies. And as he looks for his girlfriend, he can feel the branches in the timber entwine across his back and little twigs creep over his skin, searching for "gaps in his clothing, suitable places to turn inward".

I had no problem relating to that feeling because I, too, could feel the stories from the past – the tales of desperate flight I immersed myself in during the day – rousing themselves from their historic slumber, blending with the flood of refugees of the present and running me through from every direction.

Eventually, our stay on Gotland approached its end. One morning, one of our last on the island, I went down to the beach. The sea was dead calm. The long wooden jetty was being removed in preparation for the autumn and winter storms. I continued along the path, crossed both branches of the Snoder and reached the next town, Borum, where in the summers you can stay at a hostel and play minigolf. The kiosk where I liked to buy my morning paper was still open. But there was something strange about the headlines that morning. I stared at the front page, struggling to understand what I was looking at. It was a picture, a horrifying picture. It had been taken on a beach. At the water's edge, face down in the sand, still dressed in a red T-shirt and navy-blue shorts, lay a little boy: three-year-old Alan Kurdi from Syria. Black trainers on his feet. The Velcro on one of them had come undone. His eyes were closed. He wasn't moving. Around him, the waves of the Mediterranean continued to roll in, sparkling in the light of the rising sun.

There was a story to go with the picture: about how the boy and his family had left the city of Kobani in war-torn Syria and after spending some time in Turkey, made it to Bodrum on the Mediterranean coast – the Halicarnassus of Ancient Greece, birthplace of Herodotus. His father had paid close to 6,000 dollars for four seats in a rubber dinghy with an outboard motor. They set off on the night of 2 September. Their intended destination was Kos, a Greek island that to me is synonymous with vacation, summer and pure delight. Just minutes after casting off, the dinghy capsized and several of the passengers drowned. Early the next morning, they found the little boy, washed back up onto the beach in Bodrum.

I felt revulsion swelling up inside me. I wanted to scream. I wanted to throw up. Looking at the picture was unbearable – but I did it anyway, studied it again and again. And I stared at the name of the city. What did it actually say – Bodrum? Or Borum? I felt confused. Was it here, in Borum, by the hostel and the newspaper kiosk, the little boy had been found? No, that was impossible. But when I looked at the picture again, I saw the same bay as here, the same choppy waves, the same pebbles in the sand! Yes, the picture had definitely been taken here, in Borum! And it was no longer Alan Kurdi lying there, face down in the sand. No, it was the German sergeant. It was the Latvian girl. It was the refugee children from Fredrik's nightmare. They all lay there, lifeless on the beach in Borum.

I was in a daze for the rest of the day. I felt strangely cold. The damp sea air made my face clammy. My ears were ringing as I crossed the heath and the two branches of the Snoder, passing the beached jetty. As I was now walking into the wind, I couldn't help but notice a pungent odour that suffused the landscape, an acrid smell that seemed out of place among the fresher fragrances of the beach vegetation and the sea: it was the reek of rotting seaweed. When I reached the water, I realised the beach was covered in it. I took off my sandals and walked into the revolting sludge. Took a few steps through the decay. It gleamed the same shade of purple Caspar David Friedrich used in his paintings to symbolise death.

Later, I would realise I was hardly the only one who had reacted strongly to the picture of Alan Kurdi. It caused a public outcry and changed the course of the refugee debate. "It's our human decency that lies dead on that beach," someone wrote. Presidents and ministers cried. Charities saw a huge increase in donations. Businessmen and celebrities opened their wallets to put an end to the suffering. Across Europe, train stations were no longer overwhelmed by refugees alone, but also by volunteers who had come to help.

Eventually, as the flood of refugees refused to slow, attitudes would harden – but for a few surreal weeks, it was as though this was the only thing that existed: the dead little boy on the beach and our urge to help. It took a picture like the one of Alan Kurdi to awaken our empathy. There were different theories as to what made it so unique. Some pointed to the little boy's clothes and shoes. "Millions of people the world over have dressed their own children just like that," someone said. "Identification hits us like a punch in the gut." Others said what had moved them was that the boy looked so alive, even though he was dead. Or that he didn't look like what a refugee "should" look like – because Alan Kurdi wasn't "a dirty child with ragged clothes"; he was white, clean, well-dressed.

But what really caused our powerful collective reaction was, of course, that the picture had been taken at the edge the sea, that the boy lay dead on a sandy beach. No other setting would have had the same impact. Because in the twenty-first century, the seashore remains a place that more than any other reminds us of the fragility of our existence, that everything can fall apart at any moment. That humans are "merely one form among many, which the world produces over and over again, not only in everything that lives but also in everything that does not live, drawn in sand, stone and water."

12

Islam of the Sea

One of the best chapters in Ryszard Kapuściński's autobiographical book *Travels with Herodotus* is about the 1965 coup d'état in Algeria. Thanks to a tip-off, Kapuściński was on the scene just an hour or so after the nocturnal arrest of the president. He found himself at the heart of the unfolding political drama. At the same time, he was delighted to discover the city of Algiers, so picturesquely situated on the shores of the Mediterranean. He was fascinated by the ongoing meeting of Christian and Muslim culture. One is "inevitably moving in the shadow of either a church or a mosque," he writes. He also quickly became aware of the tensions between the different branches of Islam. These tensions seemed to be the root cause of the coup. Kapuściński claims Algeria's internal political conflicts – the ones that cleared the path for coup leader Boumédiène – can be explained by "a conflict at the very heart of Islam, between its open, dialectical – I would even venture to say 'Mediterranean' – current and its other, inward-looking one, born of a sense of uncertainty and confusion vis-à-vis the contemporary world." The latter tendency is represented by the fundamentalists.

Algiers, Kapuściński writes, turns its face to the sea. "But right behind the city, on its other side, lies a vast desert province that is called 'the *bled*' here, a territory claimed by peoples professing allegiance to the laws of an old, rigidly introverted Islam." Algiers is thus located in the borderland between what locals call the "Islam of the desert" and the "Islam of the sea".

> The first is the religion practiced by warlike nomadic tribes struggling to survive in one of the world's most hostile environments, the Sahara. The second Islam is the faith of merchants, itinerant peddlers, people of the road and of the bazaar, for whom openness, compromise, and exchange are not only beneficial to trade, but necessary to life itself.

There can be no doubt which of the two versions Kapuściński favours.

When westerners talk about Islam and Muslim culture nowadays, they're usually referring to Muslims of the desert. After all, Islam was founded in the desert cities of Mecca and Medina, far from the sea. Today, many majority Muslim countries in the Maghreb, the Middle East and Central Asia are characterised by their vicinity to the desert. Practically all the deserts of the Old World – from the Sahara to the Taklamakan – are still dominated by Islam. When we think about Islamist fundamentalists and terror organisations like al-Qaida and Islamic State, we picture desert warriors. To Islamists, the sea is a threat. The desert, on the other hand, is an ally. It provides a refuge for jihadists when danger looms. The desert is safety. And it has been since the time of the prophet Muhammad. Several of the caliphs of early Islam were suspicious of the sea – and not just from the perspective of military strategy, but also out of fear that the sea would "corrupt" the faithful. The sea, some claimed, was an unnatural element for a true Muslim. In seaports, they risked coming into contact with – and being influenced by – infidels. Seafaring was a poor fit for the wisdom of the Quran; the life of a sailor often required extreme improvisation and experimentation, to an extent that seemed to challenge the strict rules of personal behaviour required by the faithful.

But that's just one half of the story. Because Muhammad's new religion would in time come to spread far beyond the deserts. Muslim conquerors, missionaries and merchants may have dreaded the sea, but they also embraced it. Many Muslims became skilled shipwrights and seafarers – without faltering in their faith. Religious leaders promoted the growth of vast navies, on whose keels the Muslim world expanded – to the Red Sea, the Mediterranean and the Atlantic coast, but also across the Arabic Sea and eastward from there. In the Indian Ocean – from East Africa in the west via India and Bangladesh to Indonesia in the east – there's hardly a fishing village today that doesn't have at least one mosque. The Maldives is perhaps the clearest example of a country that successfully combines the ubiquitous presence of the ocean with religious dedication. Like Christian Europe, Islamic culture has by now, on the whole, learnt to deal with its religiously motivated dislike of the sea.

Terrorist leader Osama bin Laden enjoyed spending time by the sea as a young man. His father was born on the

Hadhramaut coast in what is now Yemen, and later moved to the Saudi Arabian Red Sea port of Jeddah. His mother, originally from Syria, grew up in the lively Mediterranean city of Latakia. Jeddah was the centre point of young bin Laden's life; he spent the greater part of his school and university years there. Latakia was also close to his heart; as a child he visited regularly to see family, and it was there he met his first wife at the tender age of seventeen. Another favourite haunt of his was Brummana in Lebanon, known for its beautiful ocean views. It wasn't until 1979, when a series of dramatic events in world politics and his personal life made him strike out on a new, more radical path, that he turned landward – toward the barren mountains of Afghanistan and Pakistan and the sands of the Sahara.

Osama bin Laden became a Muslim of the desert.

His career was shaped by the stark realities of the Cold War. He bitterly hated both of the world's superpowers – the USSR and the United States – for their arrogance, imperialist impulses and lack of respect for the grandness of Muslim civilisation. The Soviet Union's invasion of Afghanistan in December 1979 proved the final straw. He reached out to one of his old university professors in Jeddah, Palestinian jihadist Abdullah Azzam. Azzam had recently been expelled from Saudi Arabia for the part he played in the infamous Grand Mosque Seizure in Mecca earlier that year. Bin Laden found him in Pakistan and joined him there. Drawing on Azzam's long experience and bin Laden's family fortune, the two put together an army and threw themselves headlong into the Afghan War. Bin Laden himself took part in several battles and proved that it was in fact possible to push the USSR back. Other militant Islamists were impressed by him and he became a role model to the younger generation of radical Muslims. When the USSR finally withdrew from Afghanistan in February 1989, bin Laden returned to Saudi Arabia.

Sometime before that, he had, together with Azzam and a couple of Egyptian Islamist leaders, formed al-Qaida, an organisation whose stated goal was "to lift the word of God, to make His religion victorious". The plan was to build on their achievements in Afghanistan by taking the holy war to other parts of the world. But by now, bin Laden's radicalism had put him on a collision course with the Saudi government, which had agreed to let the US – the other hateful superpower – use Saudi territory for its military operations during the Gulf War of 1990. He was expelled from Saudi Arabia in 1992. He left the country and set up camp in Sudan instead. When the US intelligence services learned that he had likely been involved in a plot to assassinate Egyptian President Hosni Mubarak and was now building a "training camp" in the Sahara, he quickly became a person of interest. In the end, Sudan expelled him, too. Bin Laden returned to Afghanistan, where he settled in the city of Jalalabad. Three hundred faithful jihadists followed him there.

In August 1996, three months after his arrival in Afghanistan, Osama bin Laden declared "war" on the US, which through its continued military presence in Saudi Arabia he claimed was "occupying the land of the two holy cities". Once again, the bin Laden family fortune came in handy as it enabled him to take over an airline, which then transported al-Qaida's terrorists all over the world in the service of holy war. Throughout the 1990s, bin Laden supported jihadists in Afghanistan, Algeria and Egypt. In February 1998, he ratcheted up the pressure on the US by publishing a fatwa that declared it "an individual duty for every Muslim" to kill Americans. After the attacks on the US embassies in Dar es Salaam and Nairobi in August that same year, bin Laden was placed on the FBI's infamous list of the world's ten most wanted. Three years later, the most heinous of all terrorist attacks took place: the 9/11 attacks in the US, in which almost 3,000 people were killed.

Over the next decade, Osama bin Laden managed to evade the infidels by hiding in the arid mountain regions of Central Asia. He was now more a Muslim of the desert than ever. But somewhere inside him, at least that's how I imagine it, the sea still murmured. Surely, he missed the beaches of his youth, remembered their smells and salt, the balmy evenings, the cool breeze. The sea was so far away – and yet felt so near! Perhaps it was a premonition of what was to come. For years, he eluded his fate. But at the end of April 2011, his time had come. That was when the US launched a top-secret operation code-named "Neptune Spear". The sea god was calling the terrorist leader.

American intelligence services had figured out where bin Laden was hiding: in the Pakistani town of Abbottabad. In greatest secrecy, a team of Navy SEALs was dispatched. Just before midnight on 2 May, they stormed bin Laden's house. They found him and shot him. The next morning, his body was flown out to aircraft carrier USS Carl Vinson, which was stationed in the Arabic Sea. There, it was washed and "wrapped in a white shroud with weights to sink it". A couple of marines then placed the bundle on a wooden board. A few Muslim prayers were read. And then the signal was given and the dead man slid out over the railing. The soldiers looked on as the ocean claimed the body.

Four years later, in January 2015, the Islamic State terrorist organisation posted a gruesome video online. A group of IS terrorists had kidnapped twenty-one Christian Egyptian migrant workers in the Libyan port city of Sirte. The video showed the armed terrorists leading their victims down to a Mediterranean beach.

There, they were forced to kneel in the sand. One of the IS men, brandishing a dagger, explained that the time had come to exact revenge on Christendom for the humiliating treatment Osama bin Laden endured:

"The sea you've hidden Sheikh Osama bin Laden's body in, we swear to Allah we will mix it with your blood."

Then they beheaded the twenty-one Egyptians. The camera never flinched from the unspeakable act. A few weeks later, IS performed a similar deed; another five Christian migrant workers – from Ethiopia this time – had their heads cut off on the edge of the Mediterranean.

The term "Islam of the sea" had been given new meaning.

The atrocities on the shores of Libya set off a wave of public outrage around the world. Videos, images and stories spread via news channels and social media. The dramaturgy was impressive. Granted, western experts determined that the images and videos had been manipulated and the murders had in fact not taken place on the beach at all, but rather indoors, possibly even in a film studio, after which the sea had been added as a backdrop. But this didn't stop other evildoers from drawing inspiration from this seaside brand of terrorism. Jihadists from every corner of the Muslim world were thrilled by the idea of spreading death and destruction in the name of Allah and Osama bin Laden on the sandy shores. Death on the beach, as it was performed in the gruesome videos, made fundamentalists in a number of countries amped up and eager to get to work. Many of them had never previously considered taking up arms. Now, they suddenly felt a calling: the calling of the sea and Allah.

One of them was a Tunisian man by the name of Seifeddine Rezgui, a to-all-appearances perfectly ordinary young man who before 2015 hardly fit the description of an Islamist terrorist. He was twenty-three years old and lived at home with his parents. He liked to dance, had a girlfriend and was no stranger to alcohol. He spent his days studying electrical

chairs. Most were foreign tourists. Panic broke out, but the young student was not to be stopped. What was he thinking in that moment? Perhaps that this was the highpoint of his life. That this was the moment that made it meaningful. He walked into five-star Riu Imperial Marhaba Hotel. There, too, he killed everyone in sight. Eventually, special forces arrived. They returned fire and Rezgui collapsed on the ground. Moments later, he was dead. He'd known it would end that way. He'd planned for it, even longed for it. He was dead, but his work was done: thirty-eight people had lost their lives, most of them British citizens. Another thirty-nine people were injured.

For the rest of the season, many Mediterranean beaches lay deserted. Fear of what could evidently happen kept tourists away. And then winter came. But down in Somalia, on the Horn of Africa, there's no such thing as winter. There, beaches are in use year-round. Mogadishu's public beach is named for its counterpart in Venice: it's called Liido. One night in January, five armed men crept along the edge of the beach. They moved up toward the popular Liido Seafood Restaurant, where dinner guests had just "sat down to have a meal and enjoy the sea view". The men entered the restaurant and opened fire. People fled in panic, but many ran straight at the terrorists, who mowed them down. When the police arrived, a firefight of several hours commenced, while the waves of the Indian Ocean continued to crash outside. It wasn't over until the early hours of the next morning. By then, the restaurant had been reduced to rubble. Four of the terrorists were dead, the fifth under arrest. A total of twenty-five people had lost their lives, among them two children, four and six years old, and a

group of university students. Another twenty had been injured. When the sun rose from the sea, the sandy corpses were still being taken away. Al-Shabaab, a terrorist organisation affiliated with al-Qaida, claimed responsibility for the attack.

Two months later, it happened again, this time in a completely different part of Africa. It was a Sunday in March. In Grand-Bassam, the original capital of the Ivory Coast, both locals and foreigners had made their way to the beach, drawn by the beautiful weather. It was half past one in the afternoon when the regular breathing of the Atlantic was suddenly punctuated by a series of loud cracks. The locals were all too familiar with the sound from the days of the civil war: it was machine gun fire. Four black-clad figures, armed with Kalashnikovs and grenade belts, appeared on the beach. "Allahu Akbar!" they shouted – and killed anyone who didn't understand or refused to return the greeting. Three of the men marched down the beach in a line, shooting people as they went. The fourth trailed behind, killing survivors. Muslims were spared. One of the men walked up to two little children playing in the sand. He addressed them in Arabic. One of the children fell to his knees and started to pray. He was allowed to live. The other, Christian, child remained standing. He was killed. People fled in panic. Many ran into the water. When the security forces arrived, the terrorists killed two of them, too, before they were killed themselves. Twenty people died in the attack and around forty were injured. Al-Qaida claimed responsibility.

But Africa and the Middle East weren't the only regions shaken by terrorist attacks that year. Europe was hit, too. On 13 November 2015, 137 people were killed by Islamists in Paris in what has been described as the bloodiest terrorist attack on French soil since the Second World War. Another 368 people were injured. And on 22 March 2016, just a week after the Ivorian tragedy, thirty-five people were killed in two suicide attacks in Brussels. 300 were injured. More attacks followed. As spring turned into summer, it was feared the terrorists might follow holidaymakers onto the beaches. The 2016 beach season had become a source of anxiety.

In Nice on the French Riviera lived at this time a thirty-one-year-old Tunisian by the name of Mohamed Lahouaiej-Bouhlel. Originally from a small town near Sousse, he had moved to France at the age of twenty. Like Seifeddine Rezgui, his life seemed to have little in common with the growing number of Islamists waging holy war in every corner of the world. He had married young (his wife was a cousin of his from Tunisia) and fathered three children. He enjoyed drinking. He ate pork. He was uninterested in Islam. His only problem was his fragile psyche, which had repeatedly made him act violently; more than once, threatening and dangerous behaviour had landed him in police custody. He had also assaulted his wife, who had since left him.

The separation from his life partner is likely what caused Lahouaiej-Bouhlel to strike out on a new life path. In April 2016, he began attending a mosque in one of Nice's suburbs. He read the Quran. He began to pray. He made new, radical friends. He surfed the internet and was fascinated by the beheadings on the Libyan beach. He became a dedicated admirer of Osama bin Laden. IS caught his interest and he felt increasingly fired up by Islamist propaganda. In the end, he presumably felt he could no longer just stand on the sidelines and watch while the holy war escalated. He had to act. He had to become a martyr himself.

The bloody beach massacre in his home country the year before was, by all accounts, his primary inspiration. Like Rezgui, he felt the seashore was the ideal setting for a person who wanted to spread fear, destruction and death in the name of Allah. There could be no better place because the beach was such a clear expression of the hateful wealth and happiness of the Christians. There, on the beach, the infidels had set up their arrogant paradise on Earth. There, at the heart of their summer dream, was where he would strike.

Lahouaiej-Bouhlel hadn't attended an Islamist training camp in Libya. He had no experience with firearms. But he knew how to drive a lorry. Online, he'd seen pictures of trucks deliberately running over people. He was going to do that, but on a much larger scale. He was going to launch his attack on the most festive of summer days: France's national day. And he was going to do it on one of Nice's prettiest streets: the Promenade des Anglais, which runs along the city's Mediterranean beach for almost a mile.

We know how it ended: 86 people died and 434 were injured. Like Rezgui in Sousse, Lahouaiej-Bouhlel was killed at the end of his attack, but his work was already done. And so he became a martyr, curled up in his truck outside the elegant seaside hotel Palais de la Méditerranée. When the heavy vehicle had finally come to a stop and Lahouaiej-Bouhlel's heart had stopped beating, an eerie silence followed. It only lasted a few seconds, but it was enough to hear the sound of the Mediterranean mingling with the horrifying moans of the dying.

13

Where the Sand is Lead

On the train to Esbjerg, I am reading Michael Welland's book *Sand: The Never-Ending Story*. But I'm having trouble focusing. My mind is wandering. I think back to the quiet conversations around the dinner table the night before, at a friend's house in Lund. What did we talk about? About international politics, global tensions, terrorism, nuclear weapons. About the many wars that have flared up – in Syria and Iraq, Mali and Ukraine – each bloodier than the next. What's the world coming to? we asked ourselves, and I keep turning the question over while the train carries me through the moraines of Zealand. What are we supposed to do with all these conflicts, this violence, this hate? On an intellectual level, I feel I have a reasonable grasp of it. I can see the overarching structures, the inevitable march of history and the role of each dramatic event in the so-called larger context – but in my heart I've never been more lost or less sure what lies ahead for humanity.

On the radio, they talk about the latest developments in the Middle East, about the ravages of IS, the destruction of Palmyra and the number of dead in the latest battles. I flip distractedly through Welland's book and picture the desert and the desert warriors. I see the corpses in the sand, motionless and stiff, like plastic toys left in a sandbox. The living have moved on. The wind is howling, the desert singing. Before long, the sand will have buried the dead – the same way it buried them a long, long time ago, in the year 525 BCE to be exact, when – if Herodotus is to be believed – Cambyses II's army of forty thousand disappeared without a trace in the sands of the Siwa desert. Desert sand, Welland writes, is altogether different from beach sand. You can't build a sandcastle in the desert – the sand is too dry and the grains too round, slowly worn down to perfect spheres by the desert wind. And dead bodies don't decompose in the desert; the dry sand protects them – and so they're preserved for posterity, complete with mournful, tortured facial expressions. Often for centuries if not millennia. I've seen such desert mummies in museums.

In Esbjerg, I change to a bus that, after winding its way out of the city, takes me to Blåvand, the headland on the North Sea where the Wadden Sea meets the sandy shores of Jutland. Half an hour later, I'm there. A stiff breeze is blowing in from the sea, a chilly spring wind that lashes my face when I crest the dunes. The sea lies open in the west. Down on the beach, tiny human figures move about. Their faces are hidden inside the hoods of their coats. The silent shadows of the clouds overhead glide across the damp sand. I have to walk backwards down the last dune to shield my face from the whirling sand. Grains of sand blast my jacket. Staying upright is a struggle.

I'd pictured a serene North Sea sunset. But there's no sign of the sun in the leaden sky. Suddenly, I jump – what was that unpleasant racket? I look over at the squat old bunkers half-buried in the sand at an angle.

SHOOTING RANGE – NO TRESPASSING!

a black-and-yellow sign announces. A barbed-wire fence surrounds the military practice area. And there's that unpleasant sound again: rifle fire. Ta-ta-ta-ta-ta-ta-ta! On the other side of the barbed wire, a group of soldiers come running. Suddenly, they throw themselves flat on the sand. They pull out their rifles, get into position and take aim. Ta-ta-ta-ta-ta-ta-ta! Then they race on toward the bunkers. They're shouting something, but their young voices are drowned out by the deafening roar of the waves.

It goes to show it's still alive and well – humanity's ancient fear of invasions from the sea, and of beaches being turned into battlegrounds, as they have been so many times before, from Troy to Normandy. Is there a coast anywhere in this world that has escaped the horrors of war? Where the sand doesn't hide the mortal remains of fallen warriors?

> How dear, O kings! this fatal day has cost,
> What Greeks are perish'd! what a people lost!
> What tides of blood have drench'd Scamander's shore!
> What crowds of heroes sunk to rise no more!

In 1703, which is to say exactly one hundred years before William Blake wrote *Auguries of Innocence*, Dutchman Antonie van Leeuwenhoek became the first to put a grain of sand under a microscope. A whole new world opened up before his eyes. He squinted and stared, discovering the most unexpected and peculiar details. The street outside was loud – it was market day in Delft – but to the aged scientist it was an unparalleled moment. He was transported. He took out pen and paper and tried to convey his experience. Then he sat down to write a letter to the Royal Society in London. He described the grain of sand as it looked magnified 200 times.

> You may see not only, as it were, a ruined Temple, but in the corner of it appear two images of human shape, kneeling, and extending their Arms to an Altar, that seems to stand at a little distance from them.

He saw the world in a grain of sand.

Every grain of sand, Leeuwenhoek soon realised, is unique. Anyone who repeats the Dutchman's observations using a modern microscope is liable to feel a sense of vertigo; magnified a few thousand times, each and every one looks like an alien planet, their surfaces made up of gently rolling peaks and valleys, worn smooth by powerful forces; an enigmatic, fascinating landscape you'd want to travel to and explore. A magical micro world to escape to when hell breaks loose on Earth.

I wander along the beach, listening to the rifle fire on the other side of the fence, pondering *The Never-Ending Story* – the book and film whose title Welland has borrowed for his sand book – in which the endless realm of Fantasia has been reduced to a single grain of sand. Everything seems lost. But

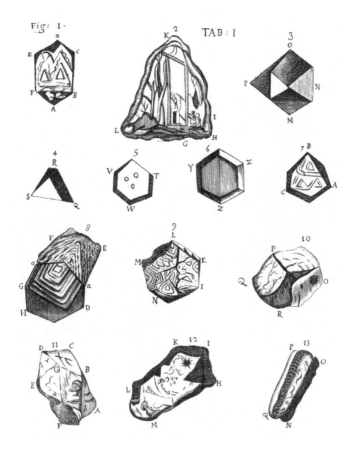

it isn't. Because in the end, this one remaining grain of sand makes possible the rebirth of an entire world.

The strip of beach the United States' 1st and 29th infantry divisions were in charge of storming on the morning of 6 June 1944, writes Antony Beevor, consisted of a flat, gently sloping, almost 300-yard-wide tidal zone and above that, a bank of shingle. Beyond the shingle, the French had built a low embankment to protect against the tide. On the other side of the embankment, the grass-covered ground was muddy. 200 yards further inland rose a steep escarpment, more than 150 feet high. The Germans had barricaded themselves at the top of this bluff.

Machine gun fire strafed the first wave of soldiers to make it up onto the beach. There were terrible casualties. Bodies rolled in the surf. "We have to get to the embankment!" someone called out desperately. But how were they ever going to make it? Crossing the beach without dying seemed impossible. Ta-ta-ta-ta-ta-ta-ta! The rifles rang out from atop the sandy heights. "It was awful," the survivors recalled afterwards. "People dying all over the place – the wounded unable to move and being drowned by the incoming tide and boats burning madly as succeeding waves tried to get in. At least 80% of our weapons did not work because of sand and sea water." A young engineer who'd gone mad with terror "started running up and down the beach until a bullet got him". Other men "lay on wet pebbles, shaking with cold and fear".

> The seas are full. The bones of men
> crowd out the bones of fish, and quiet skulls
> fall, like dice, before the gathering tide.

At around half past nine, after a few hours of combat, an officer reported that the beach was "just one big mass of junk, of men and materials." Vehicles were on fire. Dead bodies and discarded equipment lay strewn everywhere. At the same time, more bodies were being washed up by the waves, rolling "like logs in the surf". "The only people on this beach are the dead and those who are going to die," shouted Colonel George Taylor in an attempt to egg on the survivors. "Now let's get the hell out of here!"

It was time to storm Troy.

Having predicted that the allies would eventually try to invade Nazi-controlled Europe, Hitler had built the so-called Atlantic Wall – an extensive system of coastal defences that ran the length of the Atlantic coast from northern Norway to southern France. Almost a million people were forcibly recruited to build the fortifications, which consisted of long stone walls, countless bunkers and various other defences. In early 1944, when the Germans had begun to fear an invasion by sea in earnest, Field Marshal Erwin Rommel was tasked with further strengthening the wall. Hundreds of concrete mini-bunkers were built on the beaches or further inland, equipped with machine guns, anti-tank guns and artillery. Thousands of landmines and anti-tank obstacles were deployed on the beaches and various types of underwater obstacles placed in the water. Close to six million mines were buried on the shores of Northern France alone. Rommel realised the war would be lost if the invasion wasn't stopped on the beaches. "It is absolutely necessary that we push the British and Americans back from the beaches. Afterwards it will be too late; the first twenty-four hours of the invasion will be decisive." He would be proven right.

For a time, the Germans believed the invasion would take place here, on the coast of Jutland, in Denmark. Rommel therefore gave orders to deploy mines on Jutland's beaches, too. One and a half million mines were buried in the sand. Hence until the end of the war in May 1945, Denmark's North Sea coast, from Blåvand to Skagen, was lethally dangerous.

Once the war ended, the Danish army set to the complicated task of removing and disarming the beach mines. With the help of the British, 2,600 German prisoners of war were recruited to perform this "clean-up". After years of German occupation, the roles were now reversed. The mines were big, heavy lumps of iron shaped like squat, sealed tea kettles, whose lids had to be removed before the mechanism could be disarmed. Failure meant death or devastating injury. The Danes offered the prisoners – many still teenagers – free passage back to Germany when the job was done. If they did good work and disarmed six mines an hour, the whole thing would be wrapped up in three months.

Three sunny summer months in a sandy borderland of death.

All told, about 149 German prisoners of war died that summer on the beaches of Jutland. Another 165 were seriously injured. There's a film about it.

Tonight, as I wander along the beach in Blåvand, I wonder if there might not still be one or two mines buried in the sand, left over from that time, and if I'm going to step on one of them – and be blown to bits. I try to imagine that moment, those milliseconds after the accident has happened but before I'm dead, thoughts flashing through my mind even though I'm about to cease to exist. Memories of the life I've lived, the only life I'll ever live.

"The best thing to do would be to kill me, like the other," Estragon says in *Waiting for Godot*. "What other?" Vladimir replies.

- Like billions of others.
- To every man his little cross. Till he dies. And is forgotten.
- In the meantime let us try and converse calmly, since we are incapable of keeping silent.
- You're right, we're inexhaustible.

- It's so we won't think.
- We have that excuse.
- It's so we won't hear.
- We have our reasons.
- All the dead voices.
- They make a noise like wings.
- Like leaves.
- Like sand.

The Latin word for sand is *arena*, which to an English ear sounds like something else entirely. The change in meaning comes from the Romans' use of sand in the amphitheatres during their popular gladiator games – it was an effective means of absorbing all the blood spilled.

Size, Welland writes, is the only thing that defines what counts as sand and what doesn't; the diameter of the object can't be smaller than 0.06 millimetres or larger than 2 millimetres. Other than that, a grain of sand can look like almost anything – and consist of almost anything. The sand on the beaches of Jutland is almost completely white; it consists largely of organic matter. On the volcanic islands of the Pacific, on the other hand, the beaches are often jet black; they consist of tiny grains of ashes and solidified lava. In India, some beaches are radioactive; others are magnetic due to a high concentration of iron. By now, humanity has left its mark on the beach flora: plastic sand, for example, derived from the enormous amounts of rubbish drifting in the oceans, is common along many coasts. And decades after D-Day, the sand of Normandy's beaches consists in no small part of steel and lead.

When Swiss author Alex Capus in *Sailing by Starlight* thinks about Normandy, he remembers a day of jubilee in his childhood: the twentieth anniversary of D-Day, 6 June 1964. His father, who was from the region, took him to the coast that time, where military bands played and veterans in uniform made solemn speeches. That day, he sees the ocean for the first time. He strolls along the beach with his father and grandfather – in search of relics from the allied invasion. They're treasure hunters – and make all kinds of finds. They find grenade rings, shrapnel, cartridges, projectiles, belt buckles, uniform buttons, nuts, bolts, crumbling leather and rusty iron. They fill their pockets to bursting with strange artefacts. That night, back home, they sit together in front of the fire. The boy, his father and his grandfather stare into the flames while they finger the beach finds in their pockets. The large cast iron hearth plate spreads a pleasant warmth. Such hearth plates, the boy's grandfather says, sometimes conceal priceless gold and silver treasures. They're perfect places to hide treasure troves, protected by heat and fire.

Forty years later, Capus still recalls that summer night in Normandy. The war and D-Day feel remote – but he has never been able to forget his grandfather's talk of the perfect hiding place for treasure. He's now a dedicated treasure hunter. He's particularly interested in the tremendous trove described by Robert Louis Stevenson in *Treasure Island*. Over the years, he has become convinced Stevenson's treasure really exists – and obsessed with finding it. True, after almost a year spent tracing Stevenson's footsteps through the South Pacific, his search has yielded no concrete results. But somewhere, he muses, lying

14

Post-Apocalypse

History, writes anthropologist Greg Dening, was born "on beaches, marginal spaces between land and sea, ... where everything is relativised a little, turned around, where tradition is as much invented as handed down, where otherness is both a new discovery and a reflection of something old." Only by venturing down to them – and further, out to sea, toward the beaches on the other side – can cultures come into contact. Without this curiosity about what might be found beyond the horizon, behind the next headland, world history would be a meaningless concept.

But sometimes, I imagine the beach is also where the world will one day end, that it's here, with the sand tickling our toes, we will one day gather to await our doom. I can picture it, finding out one day the end is nigh. I go to find my loved ones, and we head down to the waiting sea to spend our last hours on its shores. We spread out our picnic blankets, uncork a bottle of champagne and toast the inevitable. My eyes strain to see beyond the horizon. I imagine the apocalypse will be quick, but not instantaneous: M. will point out a strange light behind the darkening silhouette of Stora Karlsö; it slowly grows bigger, forms a half-sphere, an overexposed rainbow that inexorably moves toward us. Then I see the colour of the seaweed fade and the air gets harder to breathe. I lower my eyes to avoid the blinding light – and spot a wondrous fossil in one of the beach shingles – an ancient crinoid. I think about life as it has existed on Earth for several billion years – life, which soon, mere minutes from now, will have been extinguished for good.

Nevil Shute's dystopian classic *On the Beach* (1957) opens with Lieutenant Peter Holmes waking up and scratching his back; he is sunburnt from a visit to the beach the day before. Better keep my shirt on today, he thinks to himself. His wife is asleep next to him in bed and their baby, Jennifer, is snoozing in her crib. Life seems idyllic. Peter studies the gentle rays of sunshine dappling the curtains. He relishes being the only one awake and not having to rush.

But in reality, the Holmes family, like the rest of Australia's population, are living under extreme circumstances. It's been just under a year since the end of a devastating global nuclear war. In that war, the world's superpowers detonated 3,500 atomic bombs between them – all in the northern hemisphere. All life there has been wiped out. Europe no longer exists, nor does the US, or Russia, or China. Now, the wind is slowly carrying radioactive particles toward the southern hemisphere. The holocaust is coming – and nothing, absolutely nothing, can stop it. Slowly but surely, life on the southern half of the planet is annihilated: first to fall silent is Rio de Janeiro, then Buenos Aires, Cape Town, Brisbane and finally Sydney, Adelaide and Christchurch, too. Melbourne, where the Holmes family lives, is the last big city remaining.

As they wait for their inevitable doom, the Melburnians flock to the beaches, which are crowded with people looking for a good time. More people than ever are swimming and playing in the water and sailboats jostle for space in the bay. In the suburb where the Holmes family lives, people are diving and swimming off the long pier and in the evenings, the summer parties thrown in the family's garden are set to the seductive rhythm of the crashing waves.

At first, some deny the reality of humanity's impending doom. But as communications with more and more cities further north cease, everyone is forced to accept the fate that awaits them. Radiation poisoning is an extremely painful way to die. The course of the condition is similar to that of cholera: symptoms include nausea, vomiting, and an inability to eat and eventually drink; in time, that which was once a human shrivels up and dies. The Australian government authorises pharmacies to distribute suicide pills to anyone who wants them. That way, so the thinking goes, everyone is free to decide whether they want to endure the torments of radiation sickness – or die in a more "dignified" way. Most people choose the pill.

But Shute's seaside dystopia is really an exception. Apocalyptic narratives with absolutely no hope for the human race are rare. Usually, at least a handful of people survive. And these survivors often make their way to the sea. One example is Cormac McCarthy's *The Road*, in which an emaciated father and his young son journey through a post-apocalyptic landscape. They're following an old map. On the map is a coastline. The boy, who is too young to have experienced the world such as it once was, doesn't understand what a "coast" is. But the coast is their destination. "Everything depends on reaching the coast," the father says, though he's unable to explain why. In his heart of hearts, he knows his longing for the sea is based on unfounded expectations. And yet, it spurs him on.

Dangers lurk around every bend. Hunger is their worst enemy, but there are also bandits and cannibals. Several times, they're on the verge of falling into the clutches of "bad guys". But in the end, they reach it: what was once the Atlantic. Sandy dunes rise up and beyond them, they see it: the ocean and the lead-grey beach. It's a desolate sight:

> No gulls or shorebirds. Charred and senseless artifacts strewn down the shoreline or rolling in the surf. ... The wind coming off the water smelled faintly of iodine. That was all. There was no sea smell in it. ... Glass floats covered with a gray crust. The bones of seabirds. At the tide line a woven mat of weeds and the ribs of fishes in their millions stretching along the shore as far as eye could see like an isocline of death. One vast salt sepulchre.

They make camp among the dunes. Using salt-encrusted driftwood, they make a fire and cook a simple meal. They gaze out at the sea and imagine another father and another boy sitting on the opposite shore, on an invisible continent beyond the horizon. The surf rocks the boy to sleep. But his father knows his own days are numbered. The cough that has plagued him on their journey, has grown increasingly unendurable, and now he can taste blood in the phlegm. That night, he wakes up and walks down to the water's edge, deep in thought. The fire crackles. In the film version of McCarthy's novel, Viggo Mortensen's face shimmers, like in a Rembrandt painting, in the firelight. The waves continue to roll in. But when the boy wakes up, his father is already dead.

In P.C. Jersild's novel *After the Flood*, the basic plot is similar: global nuclear war has wiped out civilisation and the few survivors live under terrible conditions. About thirty years have passed since the end of the war. Now, virtually unmitigated savagery is the order of the day and humans are animals among other animals. The sea and the coast play a central role in the worldview of the survivors. But of modern humanity's longing for the beach, nothing remains. Instead, the seashore has reclaimed its ancient role as a realm of fear and death, a territory carefully avoided. The seaweed reeks of iodine and pirates regularly raid the coast. The monstrous tsunami that swept in at the end of the war, obliterating everything in its path, is also remembered. There are still old postcards about that show what beaches used to look like – their pictures make the main character Edvin burst out laughing, because the idea of thousands of people willingly seeking out a beach – not to mention peacefully stretching out in the sun next to each other – seems so comical. Times are different now: the beaches are deserted, and the sea is synonymous with doom and evil. Edvin, who spent several years at sea, making a living as the lover of ageing ship captains, notes that people harbour an "irrational hatred of anything that came from the sea".

So much for literary depictions of the apocalypse. But there are places in the world where the apocalypse has already happened, where it's reality, not fiction. Between 1946 and

1962, the US detonated a total of 105 atomic bombs of various types and sizes on and around the Marshall Islands. It started with a "test" of a 21-kiloton bomb over the Bikini Atoll – an event that lives on in popular memory through the highly "explosive" item of clothing that has since carried the name of the destroyed islands. After 1948, operations were relocated to the Eniwetok Atoll, almost two hundred miles west of Bikini. That was where the US tested its first hydrogen bomb. It annihilated one of the islands, Elugelab. Two years later, Castle Bravo was detonated. It remains the most powerful nuclear weapon the US has ever used. Unfortunately, the explosion was more devastating than the engineers had foreseen. Radioactive particles were dispersed over an enormous area that included several inhabited islands. Over the days that followed, the American navy evacuated the affected islanders, but even so, many developed cancer and experienced foetal abnormalities as a direct result. A Japanese fishing vessel also happened to be nearby; one of its crewmembers died of radiation sickness.

This tragedy notwithstanding, the nuclear tests continued for many years, not only at the Bikini and Eniwetok Atolls, but also around Christmas Island. The American nuclear tests didn't cease until 1963, when the two feuding Cold War powers signed the Partial Test Ban Treaty. By then, the nuclear club had been joined by Britain, which announced its nuclear capability by detonating two atomic bombs on the Montebello Islands off the coast of Australia.

The British subsequently detonated several bombs on Malden Island and Christmas Island. Soon after, the three nuclear powers were joined by France, whose South Pacific empire was put to use for similar purposes. Names like the Mururoa Atoll will always be associated with this French nuclear apocalypse. France conducted a total of 193 "tests" in the Pacific. The explosions didn't stop until 1996.

In J. G. Ballard's short story *The Terminal Beach* (1964), a middle-aged man arrives on Eniwetok, the onetime Mecca of America's nuclear generals. His name is Traven. Having lost his wife and son in a car accident, he has left everything behind and set off on a meandering, aimless sea journey. After weeks at sea, he's forced to make landfall on Eniwetok when his small boat's hull tears open on a sharp coral reef. He wades up onto the beach in the dark and makes his way across the dunes, where the blurred silhouettes of bunkers and concrete towers from the era of nuclear testing appear like shadows between the palm trees. He lies down to sleep among old newspapers in one of the abandoned facilities. He listens to the waves lapping against the shore; the sound reminds him of the beach in Dakar where he was born, on the shores of a different ocean, in a different time. The world was different back then; the bombs hadn't been dropped over Japan and the thermonuclear human – Eniwetok man – had not yet been born.

The next morning, he tries to find his way back to the beach, but manages to get lost, even though the atoll is only a few hundred yards wide. He stumbles into a set of old tracks made by a large caterpillar vehicle, tracks that were made permanent when the unfathomable heat of thermonuclear explosions turned the sand into glass. He's stunned and horrified by the entirely synthetic, post-apocalyptic landscape. In a crater, he discovers what at first glance looks like a pile of human bodies, but which closer inspection reveals to be leftover plastic mannequins studied for effects during the nuclear tests. Their faces, destroyed by the heat, are twisted into strange grimaces.

Eniwetok, Traven muses, is an "Auschwitz of the soul". But something about it resonates with him, with his own fate. And so, he stays. He has nowhere else to be. Soon, he has lost all sense of time, and his life becomes "completely existential, an absolute break separating one moment from the next like two quantal events". He can no longer be bothered to look for food. Instead, he lives off old rations he scavenges in the ruins. A few weeks pass. He loses weight, is on the brink of succumbing. But his mind is made up: he's never leaving Eniwetok.

"Have mercy, my God!" sings the alto in Bach's St. Matthew Passion. "Have mercy, for the sake of my tears!" In Andrei Tarkovsky's final film, *The Sacrifice* (1986), the beautiful, angelic song eventually morphs into the dissonant screeching of a gull and the lapping of waves against a Baltic shore. Among the rocks, a father and his son are planting a tree together.

The tree of life, God's tree. It's sacred, life on Earth. For millions of years, through countless generations, it has endured. Humanity is sacred, too. But how long will humans continue to exist in this world?

That night, the warplanes arrive, roaring high above the purple sea at supersonic speed. It has finally broken out, what everyone has feared: another world war. The third one, the final one, the one that will obliterate human civilisation. In the seaside house, dinner has just been served, but who can eat now? A stunned silence ensues. The shock is absolute. The people around the table withdraw into themselves. "Can't we do something?!" someone finally shouts in despair. Outside, dusk is falling. Dew settles on the beach grass. In the distance, out of the fog in the east, comes the low moan of a foghorn. "Lord! Help me!" Alexander prays. Have mercy for the sake of my tears.

Outside, the waves continue to roll in, their crests foaming white in the hazy twilight.

15

The Flood

There was a time when sea levels were significantly – almost 400 feet – lower than they are today. For most of the Pleistocene Era, the geological period that began 2.6 million years ago and ended with the most recent Ice Age, the islands that now form the United Kingdom and Ireland were part of the European continent. Where the North Sea is now, there was once a barren tundra, which in summer transformed into a verdant steppe. Enormous herds of woolly mammoths roamed these lowlands, and they weren't alone: as the climate warmed, a diverse range of lifeforms joined them, attracted by the pleasant grasslands where lakes and rivers alternated with rolling hills and shady forests. Humans thrived here, too, grateful for the plentiful supply of food, water, and wood for both building and burning. The population grew steadily until this was the most crowded part of Europe. The inhabitants made axes, spears, and harpoons out of wood, bone, and stone. They travelled across lakes and up and down rivers in canoes fashioned from logs. They were hunter-gatherers who used dogs in the hunt. It was Stone Age life at its finest. But as the ice melted, the land was slowly submerged, until only a handful of the highest hills still rose out of the sea. And then, in the end, they, too, disappeared beneath the waves.

It has been named Doggerland, the world that was drowned by the North Sea. Over the past ten years, interest in this lost European region has exploded, among geologists, archaeologists, and historians, as well as fiction writers and artists. It's easy to see why, though the motivation is rarely explicitly stated: Doggerland's story is ours. Like the hunters of the Ice Age, we, in this era of impending climate catastrophe, have to deal with the fact that the world is warming, that sea levels are rising, and that our coastlines are retreating a little more every day. Just like the Doggerlandians of yore, we live in a time of change, and none of us knows how it will end.

Just before Christmas, 2021, I read in the paper that a play entitled "Doggerland" was going to be performed back home in Stockholm. The director was a man of Dutch extraction, Andreas Boonstra. I took the metro out to Gubbängen, a southern suburb, to see it one night. My throat felt rather scratchy at the time and perhaps I should have stayed home. The covid pandemic that had begun two years earlier was by no means over – on the contrary, the new omicron variant raged and many people around me were sick. But the Doggerland theme intrigued me. The play was based on a book, Julia Blackburn's *Time Song: Searching for Doggerland*. On stage, Boonstra and a female associate read excerpts from the book. They were trying to understand it, to understand Doggerland, this submerged realm, in relation to their own lives. And so, in a way, the play became a comment on the pandemic, which had turned their lives upside-down.

Blackburn's book was formally classified as "history", but that didn't stop around a third of it from taking the form of 18 long poems – "time songs" – which in turn were based on scientific publications. The rest of the text took as its jumping-off point conversations with people whose lives had in one way or another become intertwined with Doggerland. In the end, or so it seemed to me, *Time Song* was really about Julia Blackburn herself. She'd recently lost her husband, Dutch artist Herman Makkink, and the North Sea – and thus Doggerland – had become a site of love and grief, which through its geographical location between their respective home countries both united and, at the time of his death, separated them.

From the stage, Boonstra read about how Blackburn went searching for Doggerland in her own corner of England – the same corner, I'm tempted to add, that W. G. Sebald traversed in *The Rings of Saturn*, in search of the polysemous traces of calamity. At dusk, she walked along the North Sea shore, seeking – and finding – remains from the deep past: dinosaur fossils, mammoth bones, the petrified relics of Neanderthals. They were mixed in with Roman coins, collapsed bunkers from the most recent war, ship's hawsers, plastic bottles, fresh mussel shells. Doggerland lay tangled up in a jumble of time periods.

While the climate debate intensifies, the tidal wave of refugees coming to Europe continues to swell, and the UK holds a referendum on leaving the EU, Blackburn sits in her cottage, gazing out at the sea. She tries to imagine life in Doggerland, as it would have been during those warm centuries when rising sea levels were continually transforming the landscape. She pictures the sea rising about six feet per century, the best hunting and fishing grounds of previous generations irrevocably slipping into the realm of mourning, memory, and legend. The Doggerlandians held on for as long as they could, even as they were forced to watch the land they inhabited change beyond recognition. Sandy pine forests turned into stands of blackened bones, surrounded by churning saltwater. Campsites on the coast, huts, fish traps, mushroom picking places, oyster beds, the nesting sites of seabirds – all were at risk of being swept away at any moment. In the tidal zone, the air was thick with the stench of drowned cadavers and rotting vegetation.

They sensed they needed to do something to appease the sea. First, they did what they could to tame nature through technology and physical effort. When that didn't help, archaeological finds tell us they began to bring sacrifices to the shoreline, in the form of bone object, stone tools, spear heads. The age of impending doom became an era of spirituality and creativity, brimming with religiosity and novel artistic expressions.

And yet, the sea kept rising. The catastrophe was inevitable. How did the Doggerlandians react? Sinister archaeological remains suggest that the final years before Doggerland's last beaches were swallowed by the sea were a period of violence:

> People began to die more often
> From acts of violence to each other
> The skeletons of men in particular
> Showing fatal damage from heavy blows
> To the left-hand side of the skull

Hearing Boonstra recite Blackburn's time song was chilling; the words were projected onto a large screen on stage, as if to underscore their gravity. The parallels with our own time seemed uncanny to me, given how global warming, and the concomitant rise in sea levels, were once again going hand in hand with geopolitical turbulence, social polarisation, and brutal violence.

I tested positive for covid-19 that night. As I lay knocked-out in bed for a full week, unable to do much of anything, I let my fever dreams morph into musings about life and death. I tried to imagine what it would feel like: to have my head run through with a spear. I tried to imagine the sensation of drowning. Then I was overcome with terror at the thought of the corona virus making its way into my lungs. I wondered if I would find myself unable to breathe and end up on a respirator. I imagined the feeling of not being able to draw breath. I figured it had to be painful, the way drowning is supposed to be sheer agony.

I thought about Boonstra, drawing parallels between the sunken Doggerland and the physical isolation most people were forced to endure during the pandemic. I thought about his despair, as he had performed it on stage, at not being able to visit the Dutch side of his family. The social world of yesteryear had, like Doggerland, become submerged; the islands of its warm, familiar archipelago swallowed by the frigid ocean of solitude. I pictured the beaches of the Netherlands, the seashells at the water's edge, the jellyfish washed up by the tide.

Throughout the pandemic, the waves had continued to roll in from the North Sea, as majestic, as deafening as ever. And yet, nothing was the same, including life on the beach. I remembered how a new kind of beach fear spread around the world in the early days of the pandemic: starting in March 2020, the seashore quickly came to be viewed as a danger zone, a place where people risked contracting the new, lethal virus. It was a fear that echoed the Medieval aversion to the seashore. The authorities warned of the risks associated with congregating on beaches. Public notices were put up and beaches were fenced off, sometimes with barbed wire. Patrols were organised to make sure restrictions were followed. On the beaches that remained open, visitors were greeted by well-intentioned signs outlining how best to avoid unnecessary exposure.

For the tourism industry, this development was disastrous, and many seaside resorts fought hard to be allowed to welcome tourists back as soon as possible. That drew protests from people who felt that it was madness to reopen the beaches, that returning to normal was bound to be fatal. The Grim Reaper himself could be seen roaming the beaches of Florida in his black cloak in May 2020; it was a lawyer named Daniel Uhlfelder, expressing his disgust at what he considered the state's far too liberal, death-promoting covid policies.

There are stories that would seem to have predicted this development. Epidemics are common in the world of literature, where they're often depicted with an exactness and (sur) realism that made me shudder as I lay there, coughing. It struck me that the sea is never far away in those stories. I thought about Ingmar Bergman's *The Seventh Seal*, which takes place along a stretch of Scandinavian coast ravaged by the Black Death. I thought about *Death in Venice* and the mysterious epidemic claiming victims on the Lido beach. And of course, I thought about *The Plague* by Albert Camus, which is set in the French-Algerian Mediterranean city of Oran.

When I finally felt recovered enough to read, I took out Camus' book. I recalled that in my youth, I'd considered it an exotic narrative, bordering on science fiction, if with an existential substructure. Now, however, it all seemed strangely familiar: a closed city, closed borders, people dying in the streets. In the book, going to the beach is forbidden, as is swimming: "the sea was out of bounds; young limbs had no longer the run of its delights." And when the beaches are no longer allowed to compete with the churches on Sundays, the latter become filled to the rafters. A priest declares that the plague is divine punishment. "Now you are learning your lesson, the lesson that was learnt by Cain and his offspring, by the people of Sodom and Gomorrah."

At first, the townspeople are unperturbed. "Then, all of a sudden, the figure shot up again, vertically." The death toll rises to a hundred a week, then a hundred a day. The fear of contagion grows as the realisation that no one is safe is hammered home. And the isolation from the rest of the world is a strain. Whenever the sea makes itself known through a cool breath of wind, or the distant sound of crashing waves, it only serves to reinforce the impression that the future no longer exists.

Doctor Rieux, the well-read protagonist of the book, tries to remember what he's read about past pandemics. He recalls that "some thirty or so great plagues known to history had accounted for nearly a hundred million deaths." It's a dizzying thought. A hundred million dead. What does that mean, in concrete terms? He gazes out at the bay and

> calls to mind the plague-fires of which Lucretius tells, which the Athenians kindled on the seashore. The dead were brought there after nightfall, but there was not room enough, and the living fought each other with torches for a space where to lay those who had been dear to them; for they had rather engage in bloody conflicts than abandon their dead to the waves. A picture rose before him of the red glow of the pyres mirrored on a wine-dark, slumbrous sea, battling torches whirling sparks across the darkness, and thick, fetid smoke rising towards the watchful sky.

In Oran, the corpses are taken away at night in repurposed trams, to a crematorium that has been erected near the beach, like a sea mark. By morning, thick, suffocating smoke blankets the area. Ancient Greek history repeats itself.

Rieux himself survives, but just when he feels the danger is finally past, his friend Tarrou is ripped away. He experiences his friend's death struggle as though he'd fallen victim to a flood, or had his head run through by a spear:

> In the heart of the tempest, Tarrou was slowly drifting, derelict. This human form, his friend's, lacerated by the spear-thrusts of the plague, consumed by searing superhuman fires, buffeted by all the ravaging winds of heaven, was foundering under his eyes in the dark flood of the pestilence, and he could do

nothing to avert the wreck. He could only stand, unavailing, on the shore, empty-handed and sick at heart, unarmed and helpless yet again under the onset of calamity.

Albert Camus was one of Swedish playwright Lars Norén's favourite authors. I saw Norén once, on a spring day many years ago in Lill-Jans Forest in Stockholm, where he liked to go for a run. I still remember the sound of his breathing, his panting, among the budding birch trees of the forest, which was full of wonderful smells and cheerful birdsong. The joy that suffused that spring scene was a stark contrast to the gloom of Norén's works. I've been told that in his youth, Norén worked as an assistant director under Bengt Ekerot, who as an actor so memorably portrayed Death on the beach in *The Seventh Seal*. Norén later took to writing poetry, and eventually his own plays. He had many admirers, myself included. But others took exception to the darkness in his dramas.

In the summer of 2000, Norén began to keep a detailed diary, which he later decided to publish in book form. It was turned into a hefty tome of 1,600 cramped pages. An insane idea, which nevertheless became remarkably successful. He continued to publish his diaries in the years that followed. On 12 March 2020, the then-seventy-five-year-old dramatist noted that "the WHO has declared a global pandemic." The next day, he reflected that he himself could easily become one of its victims. He was in the most vulnerable category, elderly and diagnosed with COPD.

Isolation took a tremendous toll on him. All through that spring, summer, and autumn, he lived cut off from everyone.

He was too afraid to take the ferry over to Gotland, where he owned a summerhouse. He sat on his balcony in Stockholm, which overlooked the water, watching boats pass by. He read Heidegger and worked on a new play, which he gave a French title: *Temps mort*. He managed to avoid contracting the virus. And yet, he felt sick and forlorn. He was frustrated with the impact the pandemic was having on his life. Just before Christmas, on 20 December 2020, he wrote:

> We mustn't allow covid to become our excuse for everything, and yet it already has. I don't know how to get back on my feet and start organising. A shipwreck loses its meaning if it goes on for too long. We're almost at ten months now. There's a pale glow over the water and the buildings on the opposite shore.

That was his last entry. Shortly thereafter, he did contract covid-19. By the end of January, he was dead.

I eventually recovered from covid. And a couple of months later, just before Midsummer, I travelled to Gotland. The catamaran made the journey from Nynäshamn in three hours. I stood out on deck in the summer sun, thinking about Vineta, a once-flourishing Medieval city that according to legend sank into the Baltic Sea. What if it was still down there somewhere, waiting to be wakened from its slumber? It was an appealing thought.

As we approached Visby, I was yanked out of my reverie by a grimmer and less pleasant sight: the harbour was patrolled by soldiers and a tank was parked on one of the piers. Russia had launched a full-scale war of aggression against Ukraine in February, and this was one of the consequences. The Swedish armed forces worried that the island, so strategically positioned in the middle of the Baltic, might become the next target for a Russian invasion, or that it would be drawn into the war somehow.

I didn't drive south towards Kvarnåkershamn like I usually would, but instead set my course north, towards Fårö, a smaller island separated from main island by a narrow strait. In the past, the strait had often played an important military role, particularly during the Crimean War (1853–56), which, contrary to what its name suggests, partly took place in the Baltic Sea. Sweden sought to remain neutral in that war, but British and French ships still demanded – and were granted – access to the sheltered harbour of Fårösund. Beginning in spring of

1854, close to seventy foreign warships were based there. But the history books tell us this arrangement took a fateful turn that summer, after the bloody battle of Bomarsund on Åland. The victorious British brought back a captured Russian warship, aboard which a cholera epidemic was raging. And that was how death arrived on the shores of Gotland. Fear of contagion quickly spread through Fårösund. Uncounted British, French, and Russian soldiers perished, along with twenty locals. The victims were buried on the southeast tip of Fårö. Today, that cemetery has become a tourist attraction.

When I arrived, I discovered the verdant cemetery was idyllically situated by the sea and demarcated by heavy cast-iron chains. A sign informed me that during the Cold War, the location had fallen within the perimeter of a military training area. It testified to the fact that Gotland had remained strategically important long after the end of the Crimean War. All of northern Gotland was designated a military exclusion zone and large sections of the coast were declared off limits. Foreign nationals were banned from Fårö. The almost three-hundred-feet-wide pebble beach was still pocked by large craters made by soldiers practising grenade throwing. It was likely no coincidence, I mused, that Ingmar Bergman had a house built nearby. The exclusion zone and the military exercises had drastically limited tourism on Fårö, creating a desolate, ominous mood. Bergman was inspired by this mood, explored it in his films.

I spent several hours at the cholera cemetery, deep in thought. The pine trees dotted around the burial site filled the air with their fragrance. As evening crept in, I wandered along the beach, past the craters. Empty cartridges were scattered among the fossil-rich rocks. I rounded a point and set my course for a Second World War bunker. When I reached it, I climbed up onto it and sat down, gazing out at the sound. The water glittered in the fading light of the setting sun. When night fell, I climbed down and made a fire.

I listened to military experts talking about new waves of Russian attacks in Ukraine on my radio. Everything that happens in the world these days seems to come in waves. The pandemic had a first, second, and third wave, too: like tsunamis, sweeping in from some unknown origin, crashing over the shores of civilisation. I was reminded of something I'd read about Doggerland: that in the end, the people who lived there were washed away by a tsunami that swept everything before it – as though the slow, gradual submersion of their homeland wasn't bad enough. The giant wave was triggered by the so-called Storegga Slide, a pre-historic event off the coast of Norway, believed to have taken place eight thousand years ago.

The *Gutasaga*, Gotland's national epic, tells us that at the dawn of time, Gotland would sink into the sea every morning. The island had been "so bewitched that it sank by day and rose up at night". Eventually, the curse was broken when a man by the name of Þieluar arrived from a distant land. "That man was the first that brought fire to the island, and afterwards it never sank again." I contemplated this fantastical tale, which probably traces its origins back to the fact that Gotland was covered with water from melting glaciers at the end of the Ice Age. I caught myself wondering if that bewitchment might not strike again at some point in the future. Should I make sure to keep my fire burning until morning, just to be safe? What if it went out, and Gotland sank into the sea just as the sun came up?

I didn't sleep a wink that night. I listened to the crackling fire and watched the pale constellations of the summer sky slowly wheel westward. I felt the dankness of the sea cling to my skin. And then, at long last, I sensed an almost imperceptible light in the east, somewhere beyond the horizon. I glanced over at the water's edge, as though to make sure the Baltic wasn't about to engulf the island. But nothing happened. Everything stayed the same. The light grew steadily brighter, and soon, the birds began to sing.

A new day was dawning.

Notes

CARAVAGGIO

The Caravaggio film mentioned in the introduction premiered in Italy in the summer of 2007. It should not be confused with Derek Jarman's classic film of the same title from 1986.

The quotes from Alain Corbin's *The Lure of the Sea* are taken from Jocelyn Phelps' English translation (Penguin Books, 1995).

Lena Lenček is a Slovenian-American historian and author with broad interests. The book referred to here is *The Beach: The History of Paradise on Earth* (Pimlico, 1999).

The Bible quotations in this chapter are taken from Genesis 1:2 and Job 38:8–11.

The Seventh Seal: Ingmar Bergman's 1957 film.

"She liked to experience hardships": "Adventure that came to a tragic end Graduate liked to experience hardship," *The Herald,* 11 December 2002.

THE BEACH KILLER

"He was run through with thirty-six wounds": from the Benedictine monk Amatus of Montecassino's chronicle *Historia Normannorum*. The quotation is found in Graham A. Loud's introductory text to Prescott Dunbar's English edition of the chronicle, *Amatus of Montecassino: The History of the Normans* (Boydell Press, 2004).

"On the shore of the Adriatic": Ann Radcliffe, *The Italian, or the Confessional of the Black Penitents: A Romance*, red. Frederick Garber (Oxford University Press, 2008).

The best book (so far) about the Long Island serial killer is Robert Kolker's *Lost Girls: An Unsolved American Mystery* (HarperCollins, 2013).

MEDUSA

The Medusa story in the introduction is based on the prologue in Theresa Levitt's book *A Short Bright Flash: Augustin Fresnel and the Birth of the Modern Lighthouse* (Norton, 2013), to which I also link back at the end of the chapter.

Charles Maturin's *Melmoth the Wanderer* is available in digitised form at Project Gutenberg Australia.

Mary Shelley's *Transformation* was originally published in *The Keepsake* (1831).

The quotes from *Paul & Virginia* are taken from John Donovan's translation (Peter Owen, 1982).

"Rather like a man who looks down from a solid cliff": The Goethe and Hegel quotations are taken from Hans Blumenberg's book *Shipwreck with Spectator: Paradigm of a Metaphor for Existence*, translated by Steven Randall (MIT Press, 1997).

The account of the history of lighthouses is based on Levitt's above-mentioned book and on my own essay "Uppfinningen som fick Frankrike att stråla", *Svenska Dagbladet*, March 16, 2014.

"That was Flint's treasure": Robert Louis Stevenson, *Treasure Island* (1883).

ENGULFED

"get to the bottom of Teresa": the quotes from Adriana Lisboa's book, which has not been published in English, were translated by Agnes Broomé.

François Ozon's *Under the Sand (Sous le sable)* premiered at the Toronto International Film Festival in September 2000.

"I love the sea as my soul": The Heine quote is found in Alain Corbin, *The Lure of the Sea*.

KATABASIS

"In Cartagena, Luis says": Nam Le, *The Boat* (Canongate, 2008).

The quotes from Rilke's *The Notebooks of Malte Laurids Brigge* are taken from William Needham's translation, which is available at www.archive.org.

"One morning he received an annoying business-letter": Princess Marie von Thurn und Taxis, *The Poet and the Princess: Memories of Rainer Maria Rilke,* 34–35 (Amun Press, 2017).

The account of Boltzmann's death builds on Engelbert Broda, *Ludwig Boltzmann: Mensch, Physiker, Philosoph* (Franz Deuticke, 1955), and John Blackmore (ed.), *Ludwig Boltzmann: His Later Life and Philosophy* (Kluwer, 1995).

The account of Rilke's reaction to Mann's *Death in Venice* builds on Monika Czernin, *Duino, Rilke und die Duineser Elegien* (Deutscher Taschenbuch Verlag, 2004).

LONGING

"My God, what is this?": Kenneth D. Ackerman, *Dark Horse: The Surprise Election and Political Murder of President James A. Garfield* (Carroll & Graf Publishers, 2003).

Luchino Visconti's *Death in Venice (Morte a Venezia)* premiered in March 1971.

"You couldn't wish for a more beautiful death": the quote is taken from an article published in the German tabloid newspaper *Bild-Zeitung*, "Malediven-Konsul stirbt an seinem Traumstrand", 29 July 2015.

TERROR

The *Dagens Nyheter* article cited in the beginning of the chapter is entitled "Drömmen om Söderhavet" and was published on 7 December 2014.

"invisible continent": the quote is taken from the subtitle of J.M.G. Le Clézio's *Raga: approche du continent invisible* (Seuil, 2006). The book has not been published in English.

"This calm is unnatural": Tove Jansson, *Tales from Moominvalley*, translated by Thomas Warburton (Puffin Books, 1963).

Spielberg's *Jaws*, which I quote from here, premiered in June 1975.

The quoted short story by Malouf is entitled *A Change of Scene*. It is included in the collection *Antipodes* (Chatto & Windus, 1985).

Camus, *The Stranger*: the quotes are taken from Matthew Ward's translation (Knopf, 1988).

The account of Cook's death in Hawaii is based on Gananath Obeyesekere's remarkable book *The Apotheosis of Captain Cook: European mythmaking in the Pacific* (Princeton University Press, 1997).

"What a delusion!": Nicholas Thomas, *Islanders: The Pacific in an Age of Empire* (Yale University Press, 2010).

THE BLUFF

"He just fell": Mari Jungstedt, *Den dubbla tystnaden: kriminalroman* (Albert Bonniers Förlag, 2009). Translation of the quote by Agnes Broomé.

William Golding's *Lord of the Flies* was first published in 1954 by Faber and Faber.

"a man with an unclean spirit": The Bible quotes in this chapter are taken from Mark 1:23 and 5:2–13.

The account of the deaths at Beachy Head is based on a report in *Washington Post*, "White cliffs of Dover become prime suicide site", 7 March 1994.

IN THE TIDAL ZONE

"Then may the poorest with the wealthy look": the quotes follow Crabbe's poem in a new edition (Tradition Classics, 2015).

The Scott quotes are taken from *The Antiquary*, edited with an Introduction and Notes by Nicola J. Watson (Oxford University Press, 2002).

"People were dancing in a circle": Corbin, *The Lure of the Sea*.

"The tide, my boys!": Corbin, *The Lure of the Sea*.

The tidal death at Camber Sands: "I brought them here to be safe: Sri Lankan father of two sons drowned in Camber Sands tragedy slams lack of lifeguards", *The Sun*, 26 August 2016.

A REALM OF SORROW

"I feel something start within me": Marcel Proust, *In Search of Lost Time: Swann's Way*. Translated by C. K. Scott Moncrieff and Terence Kilmartin, revised by D. J. Enright (Modern Library, 1998).

The Balbec quotes are taken from Proust's *In Search of Lost Time: Sodom and Gomorrah*. Translated by C. K. Scott Moncrieff and Terence Kilmartin, revised by D. J. Enright (Modern Library, 1999).

Anne Lisbeth: the quotes from Andersen's tale are from the English translation by H. P. Pull (1872), which is available online at http://hca.gilead.org.il/anne_lis.html.

"I love the beach": William Boyd, *Brazzaville Beach* (Penguin Books, 1991).

"I was not in pain": John Banville, *The Sea* (Picador, 2005).

The film *Contact*, directed by Robert Zemeckis and starring Jodie Foster, premiered in July 1997.

FLIGHT

"It was a man of about 20–25": the quotes, which are taken from *Gotlands Allehanda*, 29 November, 5 December and 7 December 1944, were translated by Agnes Broomé.

The story of the Latvian girl who died on Gotska Sandön's shore follows Algot Anderberg, *Ytterst i havet: om människor och händelser på Gotska sandön* (Diakonistyrelsens bokförlag, 1960).

"Albertina was coming toward him": Kristoffer Leandoer, *Strandridare och 13 andra skräcknoveller* (BonnierCarlsen, 2000). Translation of the quote by Agnes Broomé.

"It's our human decency that lies dead on that beach": Mustafa Can, "Hur länge varar vår medkänsla?", *Svenska Dagbladet*, 7 September 2015. Translation of the quote by Agnes Broomé.

"Millions of people the world over have dressed their own children just like that": Fredric Karén, "Att släppa taget om sina barn", *Svenska Dagbladet*, 7 September 2015. Translation of the quote by Agnes Broomé.

"merely one form among many": Karl Ove Knausgaard, *My Struggle, Book 1*, translated by Don Bartlett (Farrar, Straus and Giroux, 2013).

ISLAM OF THE SEA

The presentation of Islam's relationship to the sea is based on Lawrence I. Conrad's excellent study on the subject, "Islam and the Sea: Paradigms and Problems", *Al-Qantara* XXIII, 1 (2002): 123–154.

The biographical information about Osama bin Laden in this chapter is primarily taken from Michael Scheuer's sober biography *Osama bin Laden* (Oxford University Press, 2011).

"wrapped in a white shroud with weights to sink it": Mark Bowden, *The Finish: The Killing of Osama bin Laden* (Grove, 2012).

"The sea you've hidden Sheikh Osama bin Laden's body in": Lucien van Liere, "Killing the Heirs of the Killers: Collective Memory, Religion and Violent Conflict", in Mahmoud Masaeli & Rico Sneller (eds.), *The Root Causes of Terrorism: A Religious Studies Perspective* (Cambridge Scholars Publishing, 2017).

Seifeddine Rezgui: see, for example, "Family shocked as Tunis 'break-dance star' becomes mass murderer", *The Times of Israel*, 28 June 2015.

"sat down to have a meal and enjoy the sea view": from a report in *Sveriges Radio*, 22 January 2016, "Kvinnor och barn bland offren i attentatet i Mogadishu". Translation of the quote by Agnes Broomé.

"Allahu Akbar!": see, for example, "Horror at the Beach: 22 Dead in Terrorist Attack on Ivory Coast Resorts", *Washington Post*, 14 March 2016.

Mohamed Lahouaiej-Bouhlel: see "Mohamed Lahouaiej-Bouhlel: Who Was the Bastille Day Truck Attacker?", *The Guardian*, 15 July 2016.

WHERE THE SAND IS LEAD

"How dear, O kings! this fatal day has cost": *The Iliad*, Book VII. I here follow Alexander Pope's classical translation of Homer's epic.

"You may see not only, as it were": from "Part of a letter from Mr. Anthony van Leeuwenhoek concerning the figures of sand", *Philosophical Transactions*, Vol. 24, 1 January 1704.

6 June 1944: the account of these events is based on Antony Beevor's *D-Day: The Battle for Normandy* (Viking, 2009).

"The seas are full": Pireeni Sundaralingam, *Easter 2009 – Sri Lanka,* available at https://poetassigloveintiuno.blogspot.com/2011/11/5068-pireeni-sundaralingam.html.

"There's a film about it": The film alluded to is Martin Zandvliet's *Under Sandet* (Under the Sand, 2015).

"The best thing to do would be to kill me": Samuel Beckett, *Waiting for Godot: A Tragicomedy in Two Acts.* The English-language version of Godot's play premiered in London in 1955.

POST-APOCALYPSE

"on beaches, marginal spaces between land and sea": Greg Dening, *Mr Bligh's Bad Language: Passion, Power, and Theatre on the Bounty* (Cambridge University Press, 1992).

Cormac McCarthy's *The Road* was published in 2006 by Vintage International.

Tarkovsky's *The Sacrifice* premiered on 9 May 1986.

THE FLOOD

Julia Blackburn's *Time Song: Searching for Doggerland* was published in 2019 by Jonathan Cape.

Camus' *The Plague* is quoted in Stuart Gilbert's translation (Penguin, 2010).

"We mustn't allow covid to become our excuse for everything": Lars Norén, *En dramatikers dagbok 2019–2020* (Albert Bonniers Förlag, 2022). Translation of the quote by Agnes Broomé.

"so bewitched that it sank by day and rose up at night": The *Gutasaga* is available in the original Gotlandic version and in Swedish at http://www.guteinfo.com/?id=103. The quotes were translated into English by Agnes Broomé.

List of Illustrations

14. Dirk Bogarde as Gustav von Aschenbach in Luchino Visconti's film version of *Death in Venice* (1971). Mary Evans Picture Library/TT.

15. Duino Castle after its destruction in World War I. Wikimedia Commons.

16. President Garfield's last journey: from the White House to Elberon. Illustration from *Frank Leslie's Illustrated Newspaper*, 24 September 1881.

17. Johann Zofanny's painting *The Death of Captain James Cook* (1795). Wikimedia Commons.

18. View of Hienviken, Stora Karlsö. Photo by the author.

19. James Tissot's painting *The Swine Driven into the Sea* (ca. 1886–1896). Brooklyn Museum.

20. On Rügen's shore. Wikimedia Commons.

21. By the North Sea. Photo by the author.

22. On the shores of Libya, scene from an IS video (Sirte, 15 February 2015). Reuters/TT.

23. After the terror attacks in Mogadishu, Somalia (22 January 2016). Reuters/TT.

24. Antonie van Leeuwenhoek's sand drawings. From a letter to the Royal Society (1703).

25. Normandie, 6 June 1944. Granger/REX/TT.

26. Scene from Martin Zandvliet's film *Under Sandet* (Under the Sand, 2015). Sony Pictures/TT.

27. American nuclear bomb test at Bikini Atoll. Wikimedia Commons.

28. The English Cemetery at Fårö, Gotland. Photo by the author.